IN TOUCH WITH GOD

Marie Shropshire

HARVEST HOUSE PUBLISHERS
Eugene, Oregon

Cover by Terry Dugan, Minneapolis, Minnesota

IN TOUCH WITH GOD

Copyright © 1985 by Harvest House Publishers
Eugene, Oregon 97402

Library of Congress Catalog Card Number 84-82352
ISBN 0-7369-0322-4

Printed in the United States of America.

00 01 02 03 04 05 / BC / 7 6 5 4 3

PREFACE

The substance and much of the body of this book were originally written not for publication but as a release for my innermost thoughts over a dark period of approximately seven years. Helplessly watching my world crumble and fall apart, I needed an outlet for my pent-up emotions and an answer to my questions. So I recorded my deepest feelings and prayers, along with what I felt was the voice of God in response to the searchings of my heart.

If what I received was not always surprising, the communications were distinctive enough to sustain and escort me through an otherwise impossible path, and they have been so lasting that I'm still refreshed and dazzled with wonder by the goodness of God.

I do not mean to imply that all my comfort came directly from the voice of God. He occasionally used people and often books to speak to me. But the timing was always so perfect that I couldn't help recognizing His hand. During the month that climaxed my pain, a friend whom I had never met came by my schoolroom one day, bringing a little book of comforting poems.

I realize that, having drunk so deeply from the healing springs bubbling forth from the pens of other writers, much of my writing reflects their thoughts. Without the Scriptures and the words of wisdom from others guiding me through the tempest, this book could not have been born. I am grateful for their help.

As you pass through your own dark forests, may you too be comforted as you stay in touch with God.

—Marie Shropshire

In Touch With God

Part One

He Leads Through the Valleys...

Crushed Within

Lord, *it seems the worst thing that possibly could happen has happened to me. Every fiber of my being is crushed. How can I endure the pain?*

My Child, as you lean your entire personality on me, I will heal your hurt. I know the pain you feel. Because I suffered, I am able to help you in your suffering. Having trod the path of anguish, I felt every hurt you feel. I experienced every grief known to the human race; therefore I am able to be a haven of rest for you in your time of testing.

In the natural, you cannot endure the pain, but my Spirit is within you to give you the strength you need. You, like every child of mine, have been given the power to transcend trouble. Suffering awakens your understanding to the power available to you. Nothing is impossible with me. My Spirit dwells within you to accomplish the impossible.

In the midst of your heartache and frustrations, draw upon my strength. Do not attempt to reason everything out, but rest in my love. I am your burden-bearer. Relax in me. Let my peace permeate your every cell. Rest in the assurance that wholeness will come to you.

"Come to me, all you who are weary and burdened, and I will give you rest" (Matthew 11:28).

A Stabbed Heart

Lord, *my heart has been stabbed. Words and actions of one I love are utterly devastating. I lie down to sleep, but the ache in my heart is too great. How can I go on living?*

My Child, your only consolation must be in me. "I am God, and there is none else." These words are literally true for you now. There is no other comfort. This is no longer a pious phrase for you. Through your excruciating experience these words of mine must become living reality to you.

Human love is variable, but I change not. Many individuals are saying beautiful things about my being the God of all comfort, but to countless ones the words are no more than clever intellectualisms. You have desired reality, and you have it. You are to experience a comfort which enfolds life's severest trials in all-embracing peace.

"As a mother comforts her child, so will I comfort you" (Isaiah 66:13). Repeat the words until they sink into the depths of your being. I am your ever-present Comforter. I am not far away. I will not leave you. A human comforter would remain with you a few days and leave, but I am your abiding Comforter. Feeling the need of comfort, you are able to listen attentively to my words of comfort and peace. I know every aching cell of your be-ing, and I am present to console you. A mother might forget her child, but I cannot forget you. I am your in-dwelling Comforter. I cannot leave you.

᪥ ᪥ ᪥

Deeply Hurt

Lord, *if anyone had told me these things would ever happen to me, I would have denied it. I didn't know a person could hurt as deeply as I do and still live. How can I go on?*

My Child, you must set your determination to believe every word of comfort I've ever spoken. I am your salvation. Refuse to listen to the words of discomfort spoken by your circumstances. I know your heart is broken, but trust me a day at a time. Put your hand in mine. I will lead you through this dark valley.

You are not alone. I am with you. Say to yourself until you thoroughly believe it, "In the time of trouble he shall hide me in his pavilion; in the secret of his tabernacle shall he hide me; he shall set me upon a rock" (Psalm 27:5 KJV).

In this time of trouble I will keep you sheltered. I am your refuge. Do not be afraid. I will strengthen you. Keep your eyes on me, and I will guide you. I will surround you with lovingkindness. Commit your way unto me. I will see you through. I am in charge of your affairs, so there's nothing to fear. Relinquish everything into my hands. My kindness will not fail you. You can go on, knowing that I have set my love upon you.

Lonely Deserts

Lord, *I am aware of a desert of loneliness. Even in the midst of people, I am alone. I feel like a person standing on the outside looking in. I am cut off from joy and fulfillment. To whom can I go?*

My Child, do not hesitate to pour out your feelings to me. I understand when no earthly person can. In the midst of your despair, remember that all things are working together for your good. Remember when you were a college freshman standing alone on the street corner waiting for the bus to take you to school, you sang in sincerity every morning, "Take my life and let it be consecrated, Lord, to Thee." You offered yourself without reservation to me, and you have never tried to get away from that commitment. All these years I've been doing a work in you, though you knew it not.

A life given over to me always requires pruning. You are now feeling the pain of my pruning shears. Welcome the lopping off of superfluous branches. You are being shaped for more effective fruit-bearing. Without the removal of nonessentials, growth is inhibited. I want you to find your joy and fulfillment in me. There is no other lasting joy.

"Let not your heart be troubled, neither let it be afraid" (John 14:27 KJV). I am your guide in this desert experience. Trust me.

A Cold World

Lord, *my world is heavy, cold, dead. One whom I loved so much has turned from me. To share my hurt with others solves nothing. They criticize my loved one while sympathizing with me. That only deepens my hurt. The agony is too great for me to bear.*

My Child, in tender love I see you trembling. I have not left you alone. Many times the arm of flesh will fail you. This is the time to look to me alone. I am your help, I am your hope, I am your Comforter. Your "hopeless" situation ripens your heart for blessing. So draw near to me and feel the warmth of my love in your cold world.

Lean on me and I will give you "beauty for ashes, the oil of joy for mourning, the garment of praise for the spirit of heaviness" (Isaiah 61:3 KJV). Seeing your world as dead affords you the opportunity of seeing me more clearly as life. My life is in you to bless you in a special way during this season of your trial. Later that life within you will spring forth to bless others. So enter more fully into the sunshine of my omnipotent love. Trust me and do not be afraid.

I never allow my children to be tested beyond their

ability to endure. Before your agony becomes too great, I will make a way of escape for you. I desire "that the trial of your faith, being much more precious than of gold that perisheth, though it be tried with fire, might be found unto praise and honor and glory (1 Peter 1:7 KJV).

◣ ◣ ◣

A Broken Vessel

Lord, *I often have to choke back tears, realizing I'm being rejected. But I'm disappointed in myself for wanting to cry so much.*

My Child, do not be disappointed in yourself. Accept your humanity. You are not entertaining self-pity. So do not restrain yourself from releasing the tears you are holding. Tears of emotional release are healthy. The psalmist watered his couch with his tears. Do you think I would expect more of you than I required of David?

Do you not understand that you are working out your salvation? Your new birth, of course, was instantaneous redemption, but there is much working out in the Christian experience as you mature in me. You have asked to be a broken vessel so that my Spirit may be released through you. Brokenness removes the dross. "Remove the dross from the silver, and out comes material for the silversmith" (Proverbs 25:4).

Be conscious of my love in the midst of your suffering. Remember that your body is my temple, my dwelling place. Make an altar of your heart and commune with me there.

Remember that I am the Vine and you are a branch. There is no separation. Rest in my love. Let my love be sufficient.

Shattered Dreams

Lord, *all my hopes have been dashed to pieces. Nothing shakes my despondency. I cannot escape the thought that all my dreams are shattered.*

My Child, do not be impatient. The greater your disappointment in your own plans, the greater the opportunity for your usefulness in my kingdom. Man sees not as God sees. All is not lost; it only looks so to you. My hand has always been upon you. No experience of your life has been wasted. I will redeem and use every experience for my glory and to the blessing of others. You are a chosen vessel, so do not be afraid.

Look not at circumstances, but at me. As you continue the habit of waiting quietly before me each morning, you will find guidance. I am doing a work in you. Trust yourself to me and do not try to help. Yield yourself to me, knowing that it is not my purpose to hurt you but to purify you for my service.

Cast all your care upon me, knowing that I care for you. I love you with an everlasting love which nothing can shake or alter in any way. You feel that your plans have failed, but be assured that my plans for you will succeed. "It is the Lord's purpose that prevails" (Proverbs 19:21).

Guilt Feelings

Lord, *I'm so weak. I'm allowing another person's harshness to get to me. I know that his thoughtless words spring from his own feeling of insecurity, but that doesn't relieve my hurt. The lump in my chest is so heavy. And I feel so guilty for experiencing the pain.*

My Child, realization of guilt precedes acceptance and forgiveness. But you are not guilty. You are assuming false guilt. Do not brood over past mistakes. You've already confessed them, and you're forgiven. "There is therefore now no condemnation to them which are in Christ Jesus" (Romans 8:1 KJV).

Let my love lift you and free you from self-accusation. Whatever you find in your deep mind, bring to me for cleansing and renewal. Do not fret about what those dear to you do or say. Keep your eyes on me. That's all I ask of you. I'll take care of your loved one's problems too. Trust me to redeem every situation. Do not drown in your despair. Let your tears be tears of joy. I am in charge, and you will experience victory. Let go of all confusion.

"In righteousness you will be established: Tyranny will be far from you; you will have nothing to fear" (Isaiah 54:14).

Sickening Realizations

Lord, *the blow dealt to me by the sickening realization that one I trusted has turned away is painful and confusing.*

My Child, I know how confused and hurt you feel. The pain of the blow is intensified by earlier hurts you've experienced. Many buried hurts of your childhood have surfaced, causing you compounded agony. You are re-experiencing past pains while dealing with present reality.

Healing will come about gradually as you become more conscious of my love for you. You have difficulty believing my unconditional love when all the human love you've received has been conditional, but you will grow in your understanding of my unconditional love.

You are on your way to knowing that my love is stronger than any pain you can have. Open your heart to receive my love in its fullness. Be assured that the memories which now bring you confusion and pain will one day bring you love, joy, and peace because "I have loved you with an everlasting love" (Jeremiah 31:3).

Know of a certainty that these words spoken by my prophet Jeremiah apply to you: "They will come and shout for joy on the heights of Zion; they will rejoice in the bounty of the Lord. . . . They will be like a well-watered garden, and they will sorrow no more" (Jeremiah 31:12).

Am I Unlovely?

Lord, *am I really an unlovely person? Is that why I've been rejected?*

My Child, you have permitted your thoughts to drag you down. Your soul knows you are not unlovely but lovely. In your despair, you have given your thoughts free rein and they have led you to the gutter. Use your will to discipline your thoughts to follow only an upward trail.

I created your innermost being; I knit you together in your mother's womb. You are wonderfully made. Your frame was not hidden from me when I made you in the secret place. All the days ordained for you were written in my book. My thoughts to you are precious, my Child. How vast is the sum of them! My thoughts toward you outnumber the grains of sand. I lead you in right paths.

Meditate on my love for you. You are adopted as my very own. You have been given seating with me according to my good pleasure.

Your rejection by any individual on earth cannot compare with your acceptance by me. Rejoice in my love as I rejoice in you according to my Word. I am molding you to conform to the lovely image I had of you when I created you. You are my very own beloved child.

"Rejoice in the Lord always" (Philippians 4:4).

Waiting

Lord, *I awaken in the morning and meditate on Your goodness, determined to let Your peace carry me through the day. But positively everything seems against me, and I find it impossible to feel Your peace in all this turmoil. Why?*

My Child, you are weary because your path is all uphill and you find no place to stop and rest. The sins of the world have made crooked paths filled with obstacles. You didn't create this path, but it is the only path available to you right now. It is the walk I have chosen for you for a season.

You are feeling what I felt when I walked the earth in the flesh. It isn't easy. I understand. But the road to glory, though difficult now, leads to joy. So do not be disturbed if temporarily you cannot feel my peace. Let not the absence of peace deter you in your resolve to follow me. Know that I am as near you in the screaming activities of the day as I am in the blissful quiet of the early-morning hour spent alone with me. I never put anything upon my children without first preparing them for it.

Learn to wait for me as you wait for the morning. The first beginnings of light may be just enough to discover the darkness. If you had not enough light to see your absence of peace, you would have groped on in darkness.

Trust my light to expand until it dispels all darkness in your heart and you will be filled again with peace.

"Be still before the Lord and wait patiently for him" (Psalm 37:7).

🌷 🌷 🌷

Feeling Alone

Lord, *I feel so alone. Will there be no end to my night of despair?*

My Child, I know how lonely you feel. But you are not alone. I am with you. I will never leave you nor forsake you. It is impossible for me to be indifferent to your trials. Every moment I am watching over you and caring for you.

These unwelcome circumstances will serve to reveal me and my love more clearly to you. Your spiritual eyes will become alert to see things that are more real than the visible. Your spiritual ears will become more sensitive to hearing my voice above the din of voices in the world.

Yes, your night of despair will end. But do not be anxious while the blackness seems thick and heavy. Let your spiritual eyes pierce through the curtain of darkness until you know my presence. I am not far away, but nearer than you are to yourself. I am your ever-present Light, the Lamp to lighten your darkness.

"I will not in any way fail you nor give you up nor leave you without support. I will not, I will not, I will not in any degree leave you helpless, nor forsake nor let you down... Assuredly not!" (Hebrews 13:5 AMP).

Self-Disappointment

Lord, *circumstances are so real. I see them, I hear them, I feel them. There is no escape. My hurts continue and worsen. The only occasions for peace are those moments when I'm alone with You and can be still in body and soul. It's so difficult to "be still and know" that You are God when things are going like this. I'm disappointed in myself for feeling like this.*

My Child, I understand. Every Christian has the challenge of learning not to judge only with their five senses. I am Spirit. As your spirit continues to develop, you will learn not to be controlled by circumstances. Remember that you read yesterday, "Hope itself is like a star...only to be discovered in the night of adversity."

Do not be disappointed in yourself. You must learn to accept your humanness. You are growing; do not expect perfection of yourself. You would not be superhuman but inhuman if you did not react as you are to your present circumstances. I am leading you through these events to refine you. "For all these things are taking place for your sake, so that the more the grace...extends to more and more people and multiplies through the many, the more thanksgiving may increase and resound to the glory of God" (2 Corinthians 4:15 AMP). So lean your entire personality on me in absolute confidence in my power, wisdom, and love.

かかか

Tears

Lord, *I feel like the psalmist when he said, "All night long I flood my bed with weeping and drench my couch with tears. . . my tears have been my food day and night." Yet I don't want to give in to my emotions. What is the answer?*

My Child, do you not realize that the healing of inner hurts often begins with emotion? You have noticed how often the psalmist gave vent to tears. But as he poured out his soul to me, he was able to take control of his emotions.

The dam of pent-up tears needs to break in order for release to come. Tears bottled up and denied expression cause emotional turmoil and physical illness.

Do not allow the enemy of your soul to tell you you're indulging in self-pity. You are a normal human being with normal feelings. However, you have the privilege of exercising your will to be guided by my Spirit. Seek to grow in that area.

Tears are for healing, and you can receive my comfort and joy in the midst of your pain. While your tears flow, look beyond your circumstances and know that the outcome will be good. My everlasting arms are underneath you to sustain you at all times.

"The Sovereign Lord will wipe away the tears from all faces; he will remove the disgrace of his people" (Isaiah 25:8).

Misunderstood

Lord, *when I went today to talk to a counselor whom I thought could say something to alleviate my distress, I got the impression that he has never known hurt or sorrow. He only recommended that I get busy. Then he sent me on my way so he could counsel the next person. I'm already busy and hurting. Is busyness supposed to relieve stress?*

My Child, a person who has not felt deep hurt as you have may not be as equipped to counsel you. No, activity does not relieve wounded feelings. Many people try to lose their feelings in their work. They may succeed for a while in hiding their hurts, but eventually those feelings will come seething to the surface, clamoring for attention.

The only solution for sorrow is to lose yourself in my love and wait patiently for my healing ointment to penetrate to the deep wounded crevices of your being. Be not disturbed by what man tells you. Abide in my love. Do not be tired by waiting. I have fashioned each part of your frame, and I know how much strain you can take. I will see that you have no more than you can bear. Again I say, Rest in me.

"Blessed are all who take refuge in him" (Psalm 2:12).

Emotional Strain

Lord, *I know Your Word is true. I know I will come through this trial. But what about now? How can I live today and tomorrow and tomorrow?*

My Child, I have prepared you for this hour. Do not try to see ahead. Moment by moment you are kept by my power. I will provide help as you need it. Take one step at a time, knowing that my love will not let you go. I will not release my hold on you.

Rest much. Emotional strain causes physical tiredness. Stress often causes my children to lose their sense of my presence. Do not make too many demands upon yourself. In the past you have been programmed to meet the needs of others. Now is the time to let me meet your needs and for you to fulfill some of your own desires. You have given yourself to others; now give yourself to you. Find something you want to do, and do it. I can best soothe your aching heart if you discipline your mind to find joy in all you do. Do all things as unto me.

Read only the portions of my Word which inspire and uplift you. (Save the rest for a later time.) Dwell on my love. "For the Lord God is a sun and a shield; the Lord will give grace and glory; no good thing will he withhold from them that walk uprightly (Psalm 84:11 KJV). I am your unchanging God, your refuge today and tomorrow.

Need of Assurance

Lord, *when loved ones have let me down, I need much assurance that my sorrow will not last forever. I'm still not sure I can endure this trial.*

My Child, your rest is in me and only in me. You cannot find me in people or circumstances. They are frail and changing, but I am the Lord who never changes.

Happiness is fleeting because it depends on people and circumstances. Happiness and unhappiness are caused by happenings. But joy is eternal because I am the source of joy. Therefore you must look beyond happenings and rejoice in me.

Your only means for endurance is praise. You must praise me and rejoice in me, knowing that I am more real than your circumstances. You may feel hypocritical in praising me when you are hurting, but to be obedient is not hypocritical. I said in my Word, "Whoso offereth praise glorifieth me" (Psalm 50:23 KJV), and "Through Jesus, therefore, let us continually offer to God a sacrifice of praise" (Hebrews 13:15).

You must will to praise and will to rejoice in me. Force yourself to rise above your feelings. Praise drives out despair. Joy heals the broken heart. No human experience can alter your relationship with me. Rejoice in that and let my peace flow like a river, washing out all your sorrow and replacing it with my joy. Continually praise me.

Trying to Please the Father

Lord, I'm disappointed in myself because I learn so slowly that You really are my Father. How can I know that I'm walking in a manner pleasing to You?

My Child, too much self-introspection leads to self-disappointment. Your sufficiency is in me, not in yourself. This period of time in your life is not a time for self-examination but for rest in me. When you remember the fruits of the Spirit—love, joy, peace, patience, kindness, goodness, faithfulness, gentleness, and self-control—apply them in your attitude toward yourself.

You have been taught that it is wrong to love yourself. But because I dwell within you, you love me and you love yourself. Accept my joy and peace, and be kind and patient with yourself. Being faithful to your own spiritual needs is the first step toward faithfulness to me. Be gentle with yourself. Exercise self-control in your thoughts about yourself.

The proud person desires to be self-sufficient without me, just as Adam and Eve craved wisdom apart from me. Do not expect to do anything on your own. I live within you to fulfill my purpose in you. My purpose will not be thwarted. Rest in that assurance. Affirm with the psalmist, "You are my refuge and my shield; I have put my hope in your word" (Psalm 119:114).

Yo-Yo Emotions

Lord, *my feelings go up and down like a yo-yo. For a short time I am able to see good in this situation, and then, before I realize it, my feelings have plunged to the abyss and I feel desperate. Sometimes Your Word speaks peace to me, but at other times it seems dead to me.*

My Child, you are seeing your human weakness instead of my strength in you. Again I remind you to accept your humanness. When you are weak, my strength is available to you: "My power is made perfect in weakness" (2 Corinthians 12:9).

You are climbing a steep mountain. The ascent is difficult but necessary. You are being strengthened as you climb so you may help others in their own ascent. Keep looking to me, and act only on the thoughts I give you. Continually remind yourself that I have not cast you off. I never cast off my people.

When your feelings have dipped to the valley, be sure you have no unkind thoughts toward anyone. My unconditional love reaches to all, and you must live in a state of continual forgiveness toward those who are hurting you. I will accomplish my purpose in you and in them. Walk in my way, knowing that I protect you from all evil. The seeming evil in your experience is not really evil, as you will later see. I mean it for good just as surely as the evil that came to Joseph when his brothers sold him into captivity long ago turned out for good.

Things Are Shaken

Lord, *my future looks so uncertain now. It seems as if everything dear to me has been shaken or removed.*

My Child, remember that I said in my Word I would remove what can be shaken so that those things which "cannot be shaken may remain" (Hebrews 12:27). Your life has to be built on an unshakable foundation. I am removing from you all insecure foundations to force you to rest on the foundation of me alone.

A spiritual house, in order to stand, must not be built on a flimsy foundation. Your false resting place is being shaken so that you will rely wholly on me. My love for you compels me to take away things and persons in whom you have taken refuge. When you are detached from earthly ties, you will see that I am your sure, unshakable Rock on whom you can depend at all times.

Do not be afraid of my consuming fire. Rather, welcome it. It is the fire of my love which must consume everything harmful to you. I am removing the dross from the silver, making you the beautiful vessel you are meant to be.

Although you are uncertain of your future, you can be certain of me and of my unfailing love. I hold your future in my strong hands. Delight yourself in that assurance. Trust in me and affirm: "He knows the way that I take; when he has tested me, I will come forth as gold" (Job 23:10).

        ❧ ❧ ❧

Negative Thoughts

Lord, *negative thoughts are consuming me. I feel tearful all the time. It's so depressing to realize what has happened in my life. How can I handle it?*

My Child, as my Word teaches you, I do not desert my people. You are one of my people; I am perfecting you for myself.

I am working out the details of your circumstances so that I may reveal myself to you in a way you have not previously known. Only those who willingly submit to the Refiner's fire can know me in the way you will know me when you have come through the blaze. Because of my faithfulness in you, others will recognize the greatness of my power.

Let the multitude of my thoughts toward you comfort you and cause your thoughts to turn more and more to me. As you walk close to me you will be able to draw quickly from my strength. My strength is made perfect in your weakness.

The day will come when you will say with the psalmist, "How precious to me are your thoughts, O God! How vast is the sum of them!" (Psalm 139:17).

"Then all mankind will know that I, the Lord, am your Savior, your Redeemer, the Mighty One of Jacob" (Isaiah 49:26).

Joylessness

Lord, *I'm having difficulty keeping my mind off the one who should be with me and isn't. I feel so unhappy.*

My Child, you are to learn that happiness is not in a human being—only in me. So do not seek happiness in being with any person, but only in being with me. If you are unhappy alone, your happiness with anyone else is only temporary. You are not complete in any human being. You are complete only in me.

When you are securely anchored in me, no person or circumstance can take your joy from you. You may turn your joy loose and lose it, but I have given you the power to be joyful in spite of people and circumstances. Learn to use that power.

I am life. My life is in you. Accept my life in yourself and you will find it sufficient.

I use the peculiar circumstances for each individual child of mine to conform each of you to my image. Separation from false earthly clinging causes them to cling to me, the giver of true joy, of lasting joy.

"I have told you this so that my joy may be in you and that your joy may be complete" (John 15:11).

Soon you will say, "For you make me glad by your deeds, O Lord; I sing for joy at the works of your hands" (Psalm 92:4).

Forgiveness

Lord, *is there anything I can do to alleviate the pain I feel? I know that I cannot change the situation, but how can I bear the hurt?*

My Child, you will experience emotional healing, but you will find it to be a process. Trust me day by day. Do not try to see ahead. Leave the future to me.

Back of emotional healing is forgiveness—forgiveness of those who have hurt you and forgiveness of yourself. Your hurt has marred your self-image, but to forgive yourself and others is to improve your self-image.

You must realize that it really doesn't matter what has been done to you, or how badly you've been mistreated. The item of importance is how you respond. Since I responded in love and forgiveness to all that I suffered, and since I live within you, you also can respond in love and forgiveness to those who hurt you. Let my love be perfected in you. You'll find that after you forgive, feelings will follow.

Releasing your resentments to me is the first key you need to unlock the gate leading to emotional healing and the alleviation of the pain you feel.

"Forgive and you will be forgiven" (Luke 6:37).

"I, the Lord, have called you in righteousness; I will take hold of your hand" (Isaiah 42:6).

Deeper Life

Lord, *I guess until recent years I lived only on the surface of life. I had disappointments, but no suffering such as this unending thing. Is this the way life is supposed to be?*

My Child, this is the deeper life you have been asking for. Suffering must attend special blessings as a balancing agent. If my children experienced only successes without experiencing trials, they would believe themselves sufficient without me and would remain immature. "It has been granted to you on behalf of Christ not only to believe on him, but also to suffer for him" (Philippians 1:29).

On one occasion Paul wrote that he was perplexed but not in despair. Paul suffered, but he understood that there was a reason behind it, and so he did not despair. He knew that I could be magnified in his life only if he recognized his own human frailties. Does not your suffering reveal your weakness and signify your need of me?

In all things I must be exalted. "The sun shall not smite thee; I only design thy dross to consume and thy gold to refine." Emotional suffering causes you to die to your selfish desires so that my life within you may emerge. Knowing that I am establishing myself in you, you can rejoice in your suffering. The normal Christian life is supposed to be a life of joy in the midst of suffering. "Rejoice in the Lord always .... Do not be anxious about anything" (Philippians 4:4-6).

❧ ❧ ❧

Weight of Sorrow

Lord, *I know that Your Word is true and that all things work together for my good. But the weight of my sorrow tempts me to question how it can be.*

My Child, since my Spirit dwells in you, when anything works for your good it is also for my benefit. You are in the stream of life. The sufferings you are enduring are not only for your own strengthening but are to be used later for other people as well.

I have chosen you to accomplish a measure of my purpose through you. This portion of my goal can only be achieved by your going through the fire of sorrow. Many other sufferers will come to you for comfort.

Let the words of Paul give you assurance: "Praise be to . . . the God of all comfort, who comforts us in all our troubles, so that we can comfort those in any trouble with the comfort we ourselves have received from God. For just as the sufferings flow over into our lives, so also through Christ our comfort overflows" (2 Corinthians 1:3-5).

As you continue yielding your will to mine, all shallowness within you will be destroyed and you will emerge from your cocoon of suffering with a new depth. Your compassion and understanding will provide nourishment for the troubled hearts I will send to you. Then you will rejoice in the privilege of being used in my kingdom.

"The Lord redeems his servants; no one who takes refuge in him will be condemned" (Psalm 34:22).

ᡱ ᡱ ᡱ

Awareness Through Silence

Lord, *the things that have come against me have conspired to make me feel like a helpless nobody. I know I am Your child. How can I be more aware that I am?*

My Child, the prescription I shall give you would cure all my children's unworthy feelings if they would only follow it. It is in the stillness that I not only reveal who *I* am—love, peace, provision—but also who *you* are.

You must learn how to still your body and mind in order for my Spirit to communicate with your spirit. A regular, daily time for quiet meditation and communion with me is essential for spiritual growth. The only real development comes from knowing me in depth.

Your culture has emphasized *doing* rather than *being*, intellect rather than spirit. Even many institutionalized churches have missed my highest intention for them. They have placed priority on activity instead of on stillness. Busyness interrupts the flow of my love and peace.

You cannot leap into an understanding of how to achieve inner quiet, where I speak wholeness to the depths of your being. You *grow* into it with persistent, daily practice. Not only the intellect, but the spirit worships me. Learn to control your wandering thoughts.

Direct them to center on me. Then hear me silently speak words of comfort and commendation to you. Thus you will grow in understanding that you indeed are my precious child.

"In quietness and in confidence shall be your strength" (Isaiah 30:15 KJV).

෴ ෴ ෴

Desire for Stillness

Lord, *I need more instruction on how to be still so that I may hear You. I believe my desire is sincere.*

My Child, your first step was taken in the direction of understanding how to enter my silence when you *desired* stillness. Many so-called desires are passing whims. When the desire of the heart is in harmony with the language of the mouth, the desire is sincere. The sincere desire is rewarded because it diligently seeks its object. You are seeking. You shall find.

For years you have found sustenance in the book of Psalms. You have allowed the Psalms to refresh your soul. You may go a step further. When you come to a thought with which you particularly identify, quiet your mind and gently close your eyes.

Sense my presence; be conscious of the love flowing from me to you. Pure, unconditional love emanates from my being. Drink in that love. Remain in that state of quietness as long as possible. Silence any wandering thoughts.

After several days of practicing such periods of uninterrupted quietude, you will begin to hear my voice rather than your own. "My sheep hear my voice" (John 10:27 KJV).

Patient Discipline

    Lord, *I'm trying to put into practice all You have been teaching me concerning meditation and silence. But sometimes the turmoil of my mind hinders my efforts. Painful circumstances beckon my thoughts in other directions.*

    My Child, I understand. You are experiencing a common occurrence. Meditating and stillness require discipline of the mind. Your trials render your task doubly hard, but this is all the greater reason for your persistence.

    The moment you awaken each morning, remind yourself of my love for you. Force yourself to recall the times when you have felt the comfort of my presence. Let your thoughts dwell there a few minutes. Know that nothing can separate you from my love. I am as much with you in the deepest darkness as when you most intensely felt the light of my being upon you.

    Say with Paul, "In all these things we are more than conquerors through him that loved us. For I am persuaded that neither death, nor life, nor angels, nor principalities, nor powers, nor things present, nor things to come. . . shall be able to separate us from the love of God, which is in Christ Jesus our Lord (Romans 8:37-39 KJV). Repeat these words several times a day. Eventually your heart will grasp the truth. Meanwhile be patient with yourself and trust me.

❧ ❧ ❧

Giving Thanks

Lord, *your Word says, "In everything give thanks." How can I be thankful for an uncomfortable situation like this? If I give thanks when I don't feel like it, won't I be lying?*

My Child, you must first *will* to give thanks. Your mind is will, intellect, and emotion. You are looking at the bitter circumstances of your life and your emotions are responding by making your body tense; your will is following lazily along. You have the power to reverse the order. Exercise your will by aligning it with mine. Choose to give thanks regardless of your feelings.

Thank me by faith, knowing that I am working things out for your good. No, you will not be *lying* by thanking me before you feel thankful. You will be *obeying* me. Lead with your will, and your emotions will follow.

Focus on me and on what I have told you in my Word. Would I tell you to give thanks for no reason? Turn your eyes from your problem to me. I am greater than your circumstances. Remember the words of the hymn, "There's life for a look at the Savior." To look at your surroundings is death; to look at me is life.

"Be joyful always; pray continually; give thanks in all circumstances, for this is God's will for you in Christ Jesus" (1 Thessalonians 5:16).

Hearing His Voice

Lord, *I want to be sensitive to Your Spirit, but I make such slow progress. Why can't I hear You as clearly as some people seem to?*

My Child, like all children, you received many negative messages in childhood. Being more sensitive than the average child, your "put-downs" left a more indelible imprint upon your heart than upon most persons.

Unconsciously you have promoted within yourself the concept you were given in childhood. When your parents disciplined you, you interpreted their actions as rejection. So you decided you were unworthy. You have perpetuated your feelings of unworthiness, and the unpleasant experiences of your adult life have reinforced those feelings.

Now you have the responsibility of making new decisions about yourself. Remind yourself often that you are a new creature in Christ Jesus. In Christ you have been made the righteousness of God. Meditate on it. Intellectually you know I love you and accept you as you are, but your heart needs to be made aware. Remember what I told you about making a daily practice of sensing my presence. When you have a greater assurance of my love and acceptance, you will have more self-acceptance, and you will hear my voice more clearly.

"My sheep listen to my voice; I know them, and they follow me" (John 10:27).

How Long?

Lord, *I cry with the psalmist, "How long, O Lord? Will you forget me forever?... How long must I wrestle with my thoughts and every day have sorrow in my heart?"*

My Child, you do well to cry out to me. Do not smother your feelings or think you are indulging in self-pity. Continue releasing your tears to me, and know that I see and care. Affirm my presence and rest in me until the turmoil has passed.

Isaiah 9:6 will remind you that the government shall be upon my shoulders. All areas and circumstances of your life are upon me. They are too much for you. Let me bear them for you. Relax in my love, and sense my reaching forth to take all your cares.

I have not forgotten you. I will remind you repeatedly: A mother may forget her child, but I cannot forget you. Accept it by faith. Some lessons can be learned only when I seem far away. But I am near, fitting you for a service you do not know of. So let your circumstances be anointed with my holy oil. Trust while you wait.

"They that wait upon the Lord shall renew their strength" (Isaiah 40:31 KJV).

Concern for Another

Lord, *today I'm feeling the impact of the storm in my environment in an unusual way. Will the rainbow never break through the rain or the sun shine again?*

My Child, you are overly concerned with the mistakes of your loved ones. As I replied to Peter when he asked me what the disciple John would do, I now say the same thing to you: "What is that to thee? Follow thou me." You are not to worry about what those dearest to you do or say, even if they sin against you. Release them to me. I am in charge. Do not attempt to take upon yourself a burden I have not given you.

Keep your eyes on me. I will take care of your dear ones in due time. The only way you can help in this situation is by releasing all to me. By giving in to hurt or fear, you will only prolong your darkness.

Trust me and go free. As I freely forgive, I also enable you to forgive, even to live in a state of continual forgiveness. Rise on the wings of my overcoming. Let your tears be tears of joy, knowing that all responsibility is mine, not yours. Accept my peace and joy in the midst of trial, and victory will be yours.

Know this: "God is our refuge and strength, an ever present help in trouble. Therefore we will not fear, though the earth give way and the mountains fall into the heart of the sea" (Psalm 46:1,2).

Crucifixion

Lord, *again I come as the psalmist: "Why, O Lord, do you stand far off? Why do you hide yourself in times of trouble?" (Psalm 10:1). With my intellect I know You cannot be far off, but my heart feels that You are.*

My Child, I remind you of your prayers in the past to be conformed to my image. I heard the expression of your heart to be like me. You are experiencing the answer to that prayer. So accept the answer as well as the suffering. Thus you will die to selfish desires in order to let me live more fully in you and through you.

Your trials "have come so that your faith—of greater worth than gold, which perishes even though refined by fire—may be proved genuine and may result in praise, glory and honor when Jesus Christ is revealed" (1 Peter 1:7). The pressures I'm allowing in your life are initiated by my love. The rugged path you're on is the only way to divine blessing for you. As you move into the center of my purpose for you, you will find victory. Commit your way to me and I will make your righteousness shine like the noonday sun.

"Those who are wise will shine like the brightness of the heavens, and those who lead many to righteousness, like the stars for ever and ever" (Daniel 12:3).

Refuge

Lord, *my tears are like today's rain—unceasing. I have run into my house to escape the downpour outside, but where is the refuge from the torrent of tears within me?*

My Child, first let me remind you of the cities of refuge I commanded Moses to appoint. When a man unintentionally harmed another, he fled for protection from his accuser. He had to stay in one of the designated cities until his case came up for trial. If he was found innocent, he continued to dwell in the city until the death of the high priest. If he left the place of refuge he was in danger. These cities were required to have good roads and bridges for easy access. Such cities were well-supplied with water and other provisions.

Even though you are innocent and blameless, this account is an example for you. You know your need of a refuge. I am a more certain refuge for you than those cities were for my people in Moses' day. You have easy access to me. I am a paved highway. I am a bridge. Interesting side roads beckon, but I have erected signs to direct you to the City of Refuge, where you will find provisions for your comfort.

You are tired from weeping. You are tempted to stop where you are. Keep moving toward me. I alone am your refuge and strength. Do not be afraid. I have provided a place of shelter. By faith, move in.

"He who dwells in the shelter of the Most High will rest in the shadow of the Almighty. I will say of the Lord, 'He is my refuge and my fortress, my God, in whom I trust' " (Psalm 91:1,2).

❦ ❦ ❦

Guilt Feelings Again

Lord, *I feel guilty for continuing to carry the ache in my heart. I know Your promises are sure, but I have difficulty releasing my burden to You.*

My Child, you are reacting in a perfectly normal way. But you are demanding more of yourself than I ask of you. The ache you feel is prompted not so much by self-pity as by your sense of justice and righteousness. You are burdened with the realization of another person's mistakes. So instead of feeling guilty, thank me for counting you worthy to carry the load.

Just continue to "live a life worthy of the Lord...please him in every way...that you may have great endurance and patience, and joyfully giving thanks to the Father ...for he has rescued us from the dominion of darkness and brought us into the kingdom of the Son he loves" (Colossians 1:10-13).

Go on your way rejoicing that you are considered acceptable to stand in the gap for another person. Rest in the assurance that your labor of love is not in vain. Your feelings of guilt are groundless. Your prayers are heard and will be answered.

Before you have passed through this valley, you will say with Habakkuk that regardless of what comes, "I will rejoice in the Lord, I will be joyful in God my Savior" (Habakkuk 3:18).

Seeking Rest

Lord, *the circumstances of my life are too difficult for me to bear. They continue to worsen every day. How can I find rest?*

My Child, there is no rest outside of me. I am shaking everything which has no solid foundation so that only things unshakable will remain. Your only anchor is in me. So look not at circumstances. Meditate on my words: "Looking away from all that will distract to Jesus, Who is the Leader and the Source of our faith ...for the joy...that was set before Him, endured the cross...consider it all in comparison with your trials— so that you may not grow weary or exhausted, losing heart and...fainting" (Hebrews 12:2,3 AMP).

I repeat—fix your eyes on me alone. Look away from everything that diverts your attention from me. I am not only the fountain of your faith, but of your joy. Let the thought of my love hold you through the night. When you awaken in the morning, again fix your eyes on me. Inhale my peace. Let that peace carry you through the day.

I will strengthen and sustain you so that you may say, "My heart is glad and my tongue rejoices; my body also will rest secure" (Psalm 16:9).

Strain

Lord, *now I'm having trouble sleeping. I'm tired but unable to sleep. I don't know how long my body can take this.*

My Child, your body and mind are cooperating with each other. The strain on your emotions is being felt by your body. Though you do not realize it, you are becoming a more integrated person. All things are still working together for your good. Circumstances are not as bad as you think. My eye is still upon you. I know your frailties and your strengths.

If you were a newborn infant I would shelter you from this storm, but I am permitting trials and testing so you may grow in spiritual stature. So cling helplessly to me as a grape clings to the vine until it is ripe. Do not be afraid.

My strength flows to you as the sap flows through the vine to the grapes on the branches. You will not be given more than you can bear. The day will come when you will be a strength to other troubled hearts. You will delight in knowing that your stored-up spiritual energy is strengthening and encouraging them. So rest, knowing that my purpose is good and that your joyful future is assured.

"A righteous man may have many troubles, but the Lord delivers him from them all" (Psalm 34:19).

Disturbances

Lord, *my moments of peace are so short-lived. If I could spend all my time alone with You, I would have it made. But during my working hours, the gnawing inside is horrible.*

My Child, I know and understand. You are learning what it means to live in the world. I also learned through suffering. But I will never leave you or forsake you. If necessary, I will send the right person, the right book, the right tape, or the right thought at the right time. You will be upheld. Keep your spiritual ears open. Be alert to my voice.

Continue to go to my Word for peace. Then hold my words of peace even at work. Let my words resound like quiet background music throughout your workday. Persistent practice of the awareness of my presence will bring tranquility in the thick of commotion.

Your future is in my hands and my love for you is far greater than you can ever understand. Put your complete confidence in me, knowing that my power to act on your behalf is overwhelmingly great. That power will be manifested on my time schedule.

Before many months your testimony will be "When anxiety was great within me, your consolation brought joy to my soul" (Psalm 94:19).

Fetters

Lord, *I know Your Word says that I will know the truth and be set free by it. Why then am I feeling so much bondage during these times of trial?*

My Child, my truth is available to all, but the amount of freedom that truth brings is dependent upon the wholeness of the individual. My truth brings wholeness, and wholeness ushers in more truth. Growth is gradual.

Have you leaned so heavily in dependence upon a person in your life that you have missed part of the freedom I came to give? In your effort to be submissive, have you looked more directly to a human instrument than to me? Have you been so "spiritual" that you have neglected to develop your whole personality? These questions are to stimulate your thinking and to show you what I prefer you to find out for yourself.

In your freedom to form your own estimate of yourself, you subconsciously have chosen an inferior self-concept. Remind yourself often that you are a new creature in Christ.

Your present experiences are temptations to let inferiority feelings feed on themselves and grow. Feed on those portions of my Word assuring you of my love and of my presence within you. When you know you can do all things through Christ, your lack of self-appreciation will be replaced by a wholesome, freedom-giving self-love.

Many chains of your bondage are now being broken simply by your recognition of them. Be grateful for circumstances that unveil fetters which were there all the time.

"He hath sent me to heal the brokenhearted, to preach deliverance to the captives. . . to set at liberty them that are bruised" (Luke 4:18 KJV).

∞ ∞ ∞

Questions

Lord, *questions still bombard my mind. Any solace I feel is disappointingly short-lived.*

My Child, for questions to bombard your mind is natural in your present situation. Do not be dismayed by the rising of questions. This indicates the presence of many disturbing memories associated with your giant hurts.

Your solace is short-lived because only recent, surface memories are being healed. The deeper hurts of your past will be dealt with later. You are demanding too much of yourself. You expect constant growth in spite of your aching heart.

Be patient with yourself during this time of recovery. A broken heart is not often healed overnight, but your heart will be completely healed. You will find a new oneness with yourself and with me. Moreover, you will find a new and rewarding sense of identity with all of life. You will realize that my Spirit has formed a new nature within you. No longer will you be impatient with yourself or with others. A new love will spring up within you. "I will repay you for the years the locusts have eaten" (Joel 2:25).

"I am the Lord your God, who teaches you what is best for you, who directs you in the way you should go" (Isaiah 48:17).

Physical Distress

Lord, *again my emotional distress is causing bodily tension. What word do You have for me?*

My Child, tension is absence of peace. Peace is "perfect well-being, all necessary good, all spiritual prosperity and freedom from fears and agitating passions and moral conflicts" (2 Peter 1:2 AMP). You have cut yourself off from the elements of peace by allowing yourself to feel hurt. Your hurt is your anger turned inward. Not wanting to blame others for your troublous times, you have poured the cup of malignity into your own being. You have swallowed anger, and your body can only suffer for it.

Let my peace saturate your spirit and sweep through your mind. Trust my sufficiency. My grace will flood you with waves of compassion for those who hurt you. As I have been with you in the past, I am with you now.

You have nothing to fear when you face everything with me. Let me live in your heart; when you think of past hurtful events remember that I was there. Feel my loving protection, my special care of you. When you have absorbed my love in sufficient quantity, you will be controlled by love rather than by buried anger. Your body will soon get the message.

Speak to your whole being, "Praise the Lord, O my soul; all my inmost being, praise his holy name.... He forgives all my sins and heals all my diseases" (Psalm 103:1,3).

Heavyhearted

Lord, *I want to believe that all things are working together for my good, but it's difficult when my heart is heavy as lead.*

My Child, I know. Until you can actively believe, simply lean on me. At this point it is impossible for you to know what I am doing. I cannot explain it to you now. But I ask you to trust me. Trust in my integrity. Trust in my character. Trust in my righteousness. Trust in my faithfulness. Trust in my nature. Instead of looking at your situation, look through it to me.

I know you cannot see ahead. Although you cannot understand, I ask you to accept by faith that your present situation is a blessing in disguise. Recognize that your heavy heart is my means of coming to you in a new manifestation of myself. You cannot yet believe as fully as you would like, but even in the dark you can lean on me. Your spirit is clouded by your negative outlook. As you lean on me, I will empower you to change your negative feelings to a joyful trust in me. Eventually your trust will grow to a strong belief which says, "My God turns my darkness into light."

For the present, know that your suffering is not in vain. Nothing I permit is wasted. Your sorrows as well as your joys are cords binding you to my love. View your problems as opportunities to practice seeing me in the center of everything. Surrendered to me, every pain serves to further your progress in my kingdom. Dare to believe that you can exchange your spirit of heaviness for a garment of praise.

" 'I know the plans I have for you,' declares the Lord, 'plans to prosper you and not to harm you, plans to give you hope and a future' " (Jeremiah 29:11).

∂ ∂ ∂

Truth in the Heart

Lord, *with my intellect I know that all Your promises are true. "I know that you can do all things; no plan of yours can be thwarted" (Job 42:4). But I've had enough of intellectualizing and theory. How do I get the message from my intellect to my heart? I want to be controlled by truth.*

My Child, you took the first step when you realized that your past teaching was little more than head knowledge. For truth to become experiential, you must live it in my power.

You are learning the truth expressed in the anonymously written book, *Christ in You:* "There is a quality of suffering that effects the highest good, that suffering which brings into activity the three great principles of growth—faith, hope, and love. The highest good is known by its opposite, and every experience can be used for ultimate good. Learn that the beauty of the morning is known because of the darkness of the night. Sorrow is ever making channels for joy."

For my truth to move from your head to your heart, you must practice a daily time of stillness. Turn from outward appearances and let my voice speak affirmations to your spirit. Silence the voice of the senses. Let my truth receive recognition deep within you. Allow my spiritual atmosphere to enfold you. When your senses suggest doubt, meet the suggestion with affirmations of faith. Desiring to be controlled by truth, you shall be.

"Who, then, is the man that fears the Lord? He will instruct him in the way chosen for him" (Psalm 25:12).

Shadows

Lord, *I look for light but find only shadows. I look for a clear path but grope about in a maze. Will the sun never shine again?*

My Child, the pain you feel gives you the impression that you are walking in darkness when you are not. The entrance of my words gives light, and you have received my words. This is not a time to cast about for answers but a time for resting in me. View this as a special waiting time, even as the rosebud quietly awaits its opening into the fully-blossomed rose.

My Word is a lamp to your feet and a light to your path. Although you are unable to see the light in your present affairs, it is there. All things happen for a purpose. Trust me. Know that I am with you. In due time you will see through the clouds to brilliant skies. I never permit my children to remain overly long in the shadows.

You are looking outside for illumination, but my light shines within you. Turn your focus from the ups and downs. Find your joy in me.

"Who is among you that feareth the Lord...that walketh in darkness, and hath no light? Let him trust in the name of the Lord, and stay upon his God" (Isaiah 50:10 KJV).

Glimmer of Light

Lord, *I thank You that my path is not all darkness, that You have gleams of radiance here and there. I appreciate the uplifting experience I had in the church service last night. I surely would like to share it with some friends.*

My Child, you are learning not to tell every experience. Mary kept her concerns to herself and "pondered them in her heart." As you keep sacred experiences to yourself, there is a buildup of power. If you repeat such precious moments to whomever will listen, you begin doubting the reality of the occurrence. It loses some of its blessedness. Never speak without my guidance. The world's doubt and skepticism has an undermining influence on your faith.

It is human to want to share insights and experiences with other people, and there are a few with whom you can share. But many do not have ears to hear. Be content to share with me alone until you have my clear direction. At this time, secret fellowship is your most valuable privilege.

"The Lord is good to those whose hope is in him, to the one who seeks him; it is good to wait quietly for the salvation of the Lord" (Lamentations 3:25,26).

Your testimony can be used to meet the needs of others, but only in my timing, so be content to wait until I send you forth.

Overwork

Lord, *I'm beginning to realize that I'm never satisfied with the amount of work I do. Regardless of how much I accomplish in a day, I feel it isn't enough. Why?*

My Child, how you feel about yourself on a deep level determines your fulfillment. You feel as if you haven't achieved enough because you have not grown sufficiently in self-appreciation. You have been taught self-degradation under the guise of humility. Consequently you strive to prove your value by overwork.

As you learn to accept yourself as a human being and know that I accept you just as you are, you will stop sitting in judgment on yourself. Any external thing carried to extremes indicates an inner need. When your inner being is healed and made whole, you will find fulfillment without overexertion.

You need to "grasp how wide and long and high and deep is the love of Christ, and to know this love that surpasses knowledge—that you may be filled to the measure of all the fullness of God" (Ephesians 3:18,19). The more you relax in this love, the less you will need to prove yourself.

Your greatness depends not so much upon your achievement as upon your character and your right relationship with me. You need to know that it is not what you *do* but what you *are* that counts.

Uniqueness

Lord, *I read in* The Practice of the Presence of God *that Brother Lawrence said he was more united to You while at his daily work than when he set aside a time for devotions. Isn't this a most unusual attitude?*

Yes, my Child. But my desire is for my children to know oneness with me at all times, regardless of place or condition. One who is sure of his position in me and whose spirit is in tune with mine discovers the blessing of my presence everywhere. Every place you step is hallowed because I am there. Your human weakness and the voice of the enemy make you doubt the reality of my presence.

Brother Lawrence heard clearly the words "Leaving the first principles of the doctrine of Christ, let us go on unto perfection" and also the words "Be filled with the Spirit." The work of Brother Lawrence in the monastery kitchen permitted him to discipline his mind in order to be in continual communication with me.

But again I remind you not to compare yourself with others. Each child of mine is unique, with a unique personality and unique needs. I deal with each one according to his particular needs. You are to seek me in the way that is natural and meaningful for you. Only be sure you spend time in communion with me. I want to conform you not to the image of another mortal, but to my image.

I would have you affirm until you are sure of the truth of it: "The Lord will fulfill his purpose for *me*" (Psalm 138:8).

☙ ☙ ☙

Refuge Needed

Lord, *the words spoken by the one dearest to me cut like a sharp knife. How can I endure the pain? When will it all change?*

My Child, I know the ache in your heart. I have known all about you from the time of your conception. My love has enfolded you from your embryonic stage, through infancy and childhood, through your youth, and on until now. As I was with you at birth, so I am with you now. My hand has been continually upon you. You cannot see it, but your troubles are opportunities in disguise. Let my healing balm flow over and into your wounds and bring soothing to your inner being.

As I have carried you through past storms, I will carry you through this one. You recognize your helplessness, so cling helplessly to me for refuge.

As I hid Jeremiah when the king sought to arrest him, so I have hidden you in the shelter of my wing. Only recognize the shelter. You may feel that you have been cast into the cistern, as Jeremiah was, but you will not sink into the mire, as Jeremiah did. I will uphold you with my strong arm. You are mine. I have a purpose for your life. Fulfill my joy by putting your complete trust in me. Men will fail you, but I cannot fail you. My love is eternal.

Make this your confession: "I will take refuge in the shadow of your wings until the disaster is passed" (Psalm 57:1).

Anguish of Heart

Lord, *the psalmist expressed my heart's cry when he said, "My heart is in anguish within me . . . fear and trembling have beset me. . . . Oh, that I had the wings of a dove! I would fly away and be at rest. . . I would hurry to my place of shelter"* (Psalm 55:4-8).

My Child, you do well to continually call to me. You have learned with my servant David that there is none other to call. Your help and comfort are from me alone. I am your life's breath. But I must lead you through briars and valleys before you can soar as the dove to the mountain heights.

Relax your hand in mine and trust me to lead you safely through every circumstance. Keep your eyes on me, not on the jagged rocks in your path. As long as you yield to my leadership, the crags in the valley cannot harm you. Let me choose the path you follow, and you will have no regrets. Those who seek their own way come to sorrow. In due time those who listen to my voice will mount up on wings of a dove. Do not seek to hasten your journey. My timing is perfect.

"Cast your cares on the Lord and he will sustain you; he will never let the righteous fall" (Psalm 55:22). Later you will be used to point others to the path of righteousness because of the path you have traveled.

Love Not Returned

Lord, my will is to do Your will. I want to be loving and forgiving even though my love is not returned. How can I be sure my attitude is pleasing to You?

My Child, when you desire with all your heart to love one who keeps hurting you, feelings of self-doubt are natural. My love within you loves *for* you. When you will to forgive but are unsure of your feelings of forgiveness, do not fret. My forgiveness is in you.

You ask how this can be. You consented to die to sin and self, and even as you participate in my death, you also participate in my resurrection. You can receive so much love from me that you will not even miss the love from the one who is denying you love. The world cannot understand this, but you will find it to be true. Wait expectantly.

"Love endures long and is patient and kind.... It is not conceited—arrogant and inflated with pride; it is not rude...does not act unbecomingly. Love...does not insist on its own rights or its own way, for it is not self-seeking; it is not touchy or fretful or resentful; it takes no account of the evil done it—pays no attention to a suffered wrong" (1 Corinthians 13:4,5 AMP).

Rejection

Lord, *despondency hangs over me like a thick cloud. I cannot shake it off. The pang of rejection is acute, and I am aware of misguided people's opinions. Help me to feel Your peace.*

My Child, remember that I too was rejected. I know how you feel, but you are not alone; you are accepted by me. The enemy would make you feel cut off from my love because human love has failed you. But remember that "neither height nor depth nor anything else in all creation will be able to separate you from the love of God that is in Christ Jesus" (Romans 8:39).

I am your God. I rejoice over you with love and I will reward your faithfulness. Continue your attitude of love and compassion. The opinions of people are unimportant as long as your relationship is right with me. Do not allow feelings of rejection and inferiority to rob you of the power available to you as you trust in me. I have given you the power to rise above your circumstances. Refuse to dwell on your hurts.

Rest in me and wait patiently for me. Rest in my promises, my faithfulness, my love. Your anxieties and fears will be hushed into calm as my peace descends upon you. My peace is not as the world gives, but a peace which the world cannot understand. My peace will keep your mind and heart at rest because you have made known your request to me. I desire to bless you even more than you desire to receive my blessing.

"Blessed is the man who makes the Lord his trust" (Psalm 40:4).

Endless Night

Lord, every day looks darker than the one before. And during this endless night You seem so far away.

My Child, you must simply trust that I am with you and that I care. You are being stripped of all comforts of self-reliance and even of reliance upon others so that you may know that I and I alone am your source.

You have seen your utter helplessness to help yourself, and you have seen the frailty of the so-called help from friends. Through this, you recognize more clearly your need of me.

But you tend to identify me with other people. Since those you trusted let you down, you have difficulty believing that I have not failed you. This is natural human reaction. As you grow in your understanding, you will know more fully that your union with me is never determined by your circumstances. My relationship with you is far above your relationship with human beings.

Nothing can separate you from my love—neither things that have happened nor things yet to come.

"He guides the humble in what is right and teaches them his way. All the ways of the Lord are loving and faithful" (Psalm 25:9,10).

A Faraway Lord?

Lord, I want to feel Your nearness. I know You are near me, even within me, but why does it seem that You are so far away?

My Child, this attitude comes from two sources—your self-image and the fact that you seldom felt close to those with whom you were physically close.

Your false concept of your own worth serves as a barrier separating you from the consciousness of my presence. Since you, like everyone else, tend to interpret me by human standards, you feel that my love is conditional. You must understand that my love is never provisional, but is based solely upon my divine nature.

While human nature often judges your value by your activities, I look upon your heart and only ask you to *be*. If you could realize that surface activity counts for nothing, you would understand the truth in Augustine's words, "Love, and *do* what you like." This lack of comprehension has raised up self-appointed judges. Your sensitivity led you to accept the verdict of others while I ask you to come only to me. Come and receive approval.

"Come to me, all you who are weary and burdened, and I will give you rest" (Matthew 11:28). I offer rest from your need to look for merit. Let it be sufficient that you are acceptable to me. As you reinterpret the images you have had of me, your limitations will diminish. The prison walls erected by your thoughts will crumble. You will feel loved. Until the awareness comes, concentrate on my promises. Let your mind rest undisturbed in the knowledge of my omnipresence.

Soon you will realize the truth of Psalm 119:151: "Yet you are near, O Lord, and all your commands are true."

Overwhelmed by Troubles

Lord, *You know my troubles are real. How can I keep from being overwhelmed by them? I feel so empty, yet so heavy.*

My Child, you have taken the right course. You are facing your troubles, neither denying their existence nor trying to escape them by filling your life with busyness. Those who become too involved in outside activities are postponing their emotional healing. A cup filled with impure water has no room for pure water. It is better to be content with an empty cup while waiting for pure water than to hasten to fill your own cup with whatever is at hand.

Your emptiness and heaviness are only for a season. Rest in me. As I heard the cry of my servant David and lifted him out of a pit of despair to set his feet on a firm path, so I will do for you.

Your troubles are teaching you to sink in entire helplessness so that you may see my power at work in your behalf. Let my peace keep your mind and heart until the day of your deliverance. Then you will be overwhelmed not by trouble but with my joy and love.

"May the righteous be glad and rejoice before God; may they be happy and joyful" (Psalm 68:3).

Focusing on God

Lord, *I know I need to focus on You instead of on my circumstances. It's easy to keep my eyes on You as long as I have my Bible or other good book in front of me, but at work it's a different story. How do others do it?*

My Child, do not be discouraged. Few of my children can say with the monastery kitchen servant Brother Lawrence, "The time of business does not with me differ from the time of prayer, and in the noise and clutter of my kitchen. . . I possess God in as great tranquility as if I were upon my knees at the blessed sacrament."

No two of my children are alike. Each one grows according to his own personality. Do not compare yourself with others. Of greatest importance is that you keep yourself separated from worldly things and set apart for my use. Let there be no contradiction between your thoughts and your life. Continue making sure your thinking and your living are harmonious with each other.

Some Christians have substituted reasoning for life, and creeds for experience. Know that you are indwelt by my Spirit. As long as you work from that foundation, you can rest in the assurance that I am at work in your circumstances. Be at peace with yourself. I who have begun a good work in you will complete it.

"The Lord delights in the way of the man whose steps he has made firm" (Psalm 37:23).

Unseen Light

Lord, *yesterday the sun shone briefly in my heart, but today everything is dark again.*

My Child, yesterday's glory is never sufficient for today, but my mercies are new every morning. Your only assurance of light is a daily reminder of my light within you. I desire to be to you an everlasting light.

To those whose eyes are tuned to mine, my light never dims. But it is your responsibility to tune in. It is according to my power at work within you that I am able to do immeasurably more than you ask or think. Open the windows of your heart today and let my light shine in to heal your hurt.

Fix your attention on me and close the door of your senses. Look away from your feelings to me. Heaven and earth shall pass away, but my love remains the same. The loss you have suffered is preparing you for a greater understanding of my nature, which is love and light. Rest in the knowledge that I am in charge of your future.

Affirm with the psalmist, "You, O Lord, keep my lamp burning; my God turns my darkness into light" (Psalm 18:28). You will become increasingly aware of my light in your darkness as you progress in your spiritual path.

Inner Grayness

Lord, *the gray, cold outside perfectly harmonizes with my innermost feelings. Will I never again feel the warmth of someone caring?*

My Child, let the awareness of my love for you be sufficient for you now. Place your wounded heart in my hand and I will heal it. As surely as I spoke to the Israelites when they came out of Egypt and said, "I am the Lord who heals you," so now I say the same to you.

You feel alone, but you are never alone. I will never leave you or forsake you. I know your frustrations, heartaches, and loneliness. My call to you is to rise above self-pity. Put your hand in mine and permit me to lead you on the upward path to joy.

Do not become centered in your present situation. Your deliverance is sure. Trust me to lead you out of this wilderness of bewilderment and despair. Delight yourself in me, knowing that I will guide you in pleasant paths and restore comfort to your soul.

"Though the mountains be shaken and the hills be removed, yet my unfailing love for you will not be shaken nor my covenant of peace be removed" (Isaiah 54:10). My covenant of peace is at work within you to make you a more balanced person for my kingdom's work here on earth.

Inner Death

Lord, I'm so miserable from the treatment I'm receiving. I feel as if I'm dying inside.

My Child, you *are* dying, but not as you think. You are dying to your carnal self, so that my life and light may shine through in greater clarity. I know the pain you feel, but it will not be wasted. Be assured that there is purpose in pain.

When you were a teenager, you sincerely offered your life to me. Daily you affirmed your desire to be wholly mine and to be useful in my kingdom. I heard you and knew you meant every word spoken. What you did not know was the costliness of surrendering your life to me.

You, like most of my children, had the mistaken idea that consecration of your life meant doing a work *for* me. You are learning that it means relinquishing your life *to* me so that I may work *through* you.

Trust me. The day will come when you will be glad for all you have suffered because you will see me more clearly for having undergone these heartaches. You will say with Paul, "I count everything rubbish in comparison to knowing Christ more fully."

"I am the Lord your God, who teaches you what is best for you, who directs you in the way you should go" (Isaiah 48:17).

Incomplete Trust

Lord, *in spite of Your words of encouragement, I still have difficulty accepting my own reactions to my circumstances. It seems I should be able to trust You more completely.*

My Child, you would not be human if your reactions were not as they are under your present circumstances. I know your weaknesses but I do not condemn you for them. I am leading you through these circumstances to refine you.

My desire is for you to stop trying to improve yourself. Stop seeing yourself as inferior. Relax and let me do the work in you. I can do no more *for* you than I can do *in* you. Your yielding yourself to me in perfect trust and confidence frees me to accomplish the work in you more speedily.

Be reminded that I who am the source of your faith am also its finisher. I am finishing your faith as a cabinet-maker smoothes, polishes, and puts the finishing touches on his product. Your faith is no more dependent upon your resources than the finished cabinet is for its perfection.

Constrain your troubled spirit into quietness, look up to me, and patiently wait for the outcome of all things. Out of the quietness will arise a power which you have not yet known.

"Look to the rock from which you were cut and to the quarry from which you were hewn" (Isaiah 51:1).

Self-Improvement?

Lord, *I'm thinking of what You said to me yesterday about letting You do the work instead of trying to do it myself. This teaching cuts against what I've been taught about self-improvement.*

My Child, you have been taught much which opposes my teaching. The reason is that many teachers rely only on head knowledge instead of allowing my Spirit to illumine their minds.

As for your present concern, take another look at Hebrews 12:2,3: Practice "looking away from all that will distract to Jesus. . .Just think of Him" (AMP). When you lie down tonight, meditate on those words. Look away from everything but me. Just think of me. Let yourself be aware of my loving presence.

My purpose is that you be conformed to my image, that I be formed in you. You cannot do the work. Your part is to yield to me as I work in you. Your tumultuous thoughts only hinder the transformation I wish to accomplish in you. Still your throbbing cares, and rest.

When my purpose is accomplished you will say, "The Lord is my strength and my shield; my heart trusts in him, and I am helped. My heart leaps for joy and I will give thanks to him in song" (Psalm 28:7).

Seeking the Will of God

Lord, *in all these things I'm having to live with, how can I be sure that I'm doing Your will? The pain I feel is sharp, but I want to please You.*

My Child, anyone who desires to know my will shall know it. You need never strain and struggle to know my will. Would you hide your will from your son or daughter? Just as you delight to reveal your will to your children, so do I.

Only continue reading my Word and making it a part of your life. I have put my desires in your heart. Therefore you can rest, believing that the direction you receive comes from me. The question is not of *doing* but of *being*. The more mature you become, the more unconsciously you will do my will.

Inasmuch as you have laid down your own will, have renounced all other spiritual voices, and have determined to listen only to the voice of the Holy Spirit, you may relax in the knowledge of my guidance.

Do not be afraid of making a mistake. Keep your attention focused on me, and rejoice in me. Receive my peace and comfort.

"Who, then, is the man that fears the Lord? He will instruct him in the way chosen for him" (Psalm 25:12).

Few Understand

Lord, *I have learned that there are piti-fully few people with whom I can share my hurts. Even my close friends seem not to understand. Why?*

My Child, I have created no two people exactly alike. As I have told you before, each one is unique. Only those who have had experiences similar to yours and who responded to me as you have are able to understand.

Even reading a passage of Scripture to two people and expecting them to have the same thoughts would be like expecting two people walking in the same garden, one in spring and one in summer, to smell the same flowers.

There are many layers of truth in my Word. Life also contains many layers of truth. That is why I said, "He that has ears to hear, let him hear." Since no two people are at the same level of spiritual development, no two have the same understanding. The only way my Word can be experienced is by living it.

Your experiences with me in the midst of your trials are as idle tales to those who have not yet realized the frailty of self and the sufficiency of me, the living Lord. Many truths are for silent pondering only. You will discover more and more such truths as you move forward.

"The Lord confides in those who fear him; he makes his covenant known to them" (Psalm 25:14).

Choked-Back Tears

Lord, it seems that no sooner do I make a little progress in releasing my hurts to You than I'm hit by another blow. I'm choking back tears, wondering if circumstances against me must go on forever.

My Child, don't hold back the tears you feel. Continue releasing them unashamedly in my presence, and know that there is healing in released tears. Remember that I also felt the pain of rejection.

Lean your entire personality on me in absolute trust and confidence in my power, wisdom, and goodness. The things you are suffering are accomplishing in you a steady growth and increased experiential knowledge of me. Your insight of spiritual reality is becoming clearer and you are being strengthened for service.

I am calling upon you to exercise endurance and patience, giving thanks to me in the midst of your trials. Remember that I have drawn you to myself out of the control and dominion of darkness and have transferred you into my kingdom of light.

You will soon say, "For you, O Lord, have delivered my soul from death, my eyes from tears, my feet from stumbling" (Psalm 116:8).

Engulfed by Floods

Lord, *I feel like crying with David, "Save me, O God, for the waters have come up to my neck...the floods engulf me" (Psalm 69:1,2).*

My Child, as David cried out to me, you also do well to call to me and not to human flesh.

As the river bears the sailboat directed by the winds, so I am bearing you up and directing every motion of your life. Many boats have taken uncharted courses and have become lost. But you have put your life in my hands, and I am in control.

To you it seems that you are drowning in despair, but those who put their trust in me are safe. The circumstances you are experiencing are bathed in my love. Since the day you invited me to be your Lord, my eyes have not been removed from you. Because you are depending on me to direct your course, you will not be disappointed.

Look not at the waters around you, but to me. You will reach the shore cleansed, purified, and fitted for service in my kingdom. Then you will rejoice in me. Your discipline of faith will hasten the speed of your ship. Though your ship is tossed by waves, stormy waters cannot arrest the progress of your vessel.

"The Lord will not reject his people; he will never forsake his inheritance" (Psalm 94:14).

Sleeplessness

Lord, it is almost 4:00 A.M. I've been lying here awake for an hour, trying to sort things out in my mind. But nothing makes sense. Will You give me a word to bring me peace and sleep?

My Child, I will remind you of one phrase in Isaiah 9:6: "the government will be on his shoulders." Every circumstance of your life is to be released to me. The burdens are not for you to carry; they are for my shoulders. Rest in me and sense me reaching forth to take all your cares.

I came that you might have life, and that you might have it more abundantly. Abundant life is found in releasing your cares to me. As your body sleeps, let your spirit awaken to the realization that I am a living Christ with shoulders to bear the government of your life.

Take my promises as the most realistic truth ever given. Trust me. Let every fiber of your being immerse itself in my love. Relax in my love. Feel my peace. Meditate on the reality of my loving presence with you. Refuse to listen to any words of discomfort spoken by your circumstances. I am the divine Comforter. Rejoice and rest in my all-embracing comfort.

In a short while you will declare, "When anxiety was great within me, your consolation brought joy to my soul" (Psalm 94:19).

Heaviness

Lord, *that lump of heaviness again presses upon my chest. How can I find relief?*

My Child, you are permitting the insecure feelings of another person to affect you. The lump in your chest is an emotional hurt you must release to me. The harshness you have received from another is not for you to bear. I have borne your griefs, sorrows, and distresses. Release them to me and go free.

As I took all evil upon myself, then rose above it and ascended into heaven, so you too may rise above your present circumstances. As you have accepted me as Savior, accept me as living in you as the Overcomer. Believe that I have taken upon myself all that is disturbing you.

Since you have no unconfessed sin in your life, you can be filled with peace and joy instead of heaviness. The most important thing in the world is your relationship to me. Do not fret about what others do or say. That is my business, and I will deal with them. All I ask of you is to keep your eyes on me. When you have learned to look through happenings to me, you will no longer feel heaviness, but lightness within your heart. You will know that "you are precious and honored in my sight" (Isaiah 43:4).

Restlessness Within and Without

     Lord, *it seems that the trials I'm having in my personal life are enough without the added pressures at school. Why must affairs in the classroom be so hectic at this time?*

     My Child, the restlessness in all your outer affairs only reflects your own disquieted spirit. It is the nature of humanity to attract to itself what it has within. One who is filled with faith attracts faith. Tumult magnetizes tumult. Fear draws fear. My servant Job said, "What I feared has come upon me" (Job 3:25).

Whatever you feel within your innermost self automatically manifests itself in your outer affairs. Negative thought patterns must be changed before conditions can be altered.

Adverse situations result from faith in reverse: "According to your faith be it unto you" (Matthew 9:29 KJV). Without realizing what you were doing, you planted bad seed. Unconsciously you expect matters in your classroom to correspond to those in your personal life. When I inspired Solomon to write, "Above all else, guard your heart, for it is the wellspring of life" (Proverbs 4:23), I meant that every thought you plant in your heart will bear fruit in your life.

All chaos in your mind and in your outer life will give way to tranquility when your heart overflows with the assurance of my power and presence and the knowledge that I am working everything out for your good. Spend much time alone with me. Cultivate an attitude of joyful expectancy.

"When you pass through the waters, I will be with you; and when you pass through the rivers, they will not sweep over you" (Isaiah 43:2).

🕊 🕊 🕊

Struggles

Lord, *again I cry with the psalmist, "If you remain silent, I will be like those who have gone down to the pit." I must have help.*

My Child, you know there is always help. I am your ever-present help. Know that I am present; I am at work in your situation. Believe it, although you cannot see my hand at work. I have built a hedge of protection around you. Do not be like those who see the shadowy side of the hedge. Through the leaves of every trial, my light shines. Be aware of that light.

You are being purified for a greater service that I have planned for you. No experience or sorrow will be wasted in your life. As I am your Comforter, you will comfort others. Rest in my love, knowing that I am fitting you for future blessings to others.

Your trial will not be too long. I never put more upon my children than they can bear. Do not struggle to get out from under the load. I am with you every hour to help you bear the weight.

"I am he who will sustain you. I have made you and I will carry you; I will sustain you and I will rescue you" (Isaiah 46:4). Hide within your heart my promises of sustenance and care. Let not the enemy tell you that I am not near. I am your burden-bearer.

Deep-Seated Feelings

Lord, is it possible that some of my negative feelings about myself come from my childhood? Would my heaviness be this great from recent trauma only?

My Child, you indeed have been inscribed upon during all your life. Everyone is. That is one of the many reasons I included in my written Word much teaching on love. Children seldom receive all the love they need. This lack of sufficient love caused you unconsciously to promote within yourself a negative self-concept.

Without realizing it, you have worn an inner plaque bearing in large letters the word "Inferior." Your recent trials have magnified your feelings of unworthiness. Being rejected, you feel doubly inferior.

But the involuntary decisions you made about yourself can be changed. Change requires persistence. Begin and end each day with the reminder that I affectionately care for you. Remember that before I made the world I chose you to be my very own. I decided then to make you holy in my eyes, covered with my love.

Get in the habit of forming a new image of yourself. See yourself the way you want to be—loving, accepted and accepting, outgoing, blessing yourself and others. This is your desire, but desire is not enough, for your faith must equal your desire. More and more you need to accept my gift of self-worth.

"So then, just as you received Christ Jesus as Lord, continue to live in him, rooted and built up in him, strengthened in the faith as you were taught" (Colossians 2:6,7).

🎃 🎃 🎃

Being Conformed
to His Image

Lord, *I don't understand what I'm experiencing. This is not what I expected from a deeper relationship with You. Evidently I was misinformed.*

My Child, you *were* misled. A great deal of instruction leaves many important truths untaught and its disciples unprepared for crises. That is why the words of my Book are necessary daily food. "Man does not live on bread alone, but on every word that comes from the mouth of God" (Matthew 4:4).

Anyone moving forward with me must go through emotional suffering. Consider that you are sharing in my suffering, as did the apostle Paul, who said, "I want to know Christ and the power of his resurrection and the fellowship of sharing in his sufferings, becoming like him" (Philippians 3:10).

Your trials are conforming you to the image of myself. When you have come forth, you will be equipped for service. This is part of my plan. I need servants who have endured the flame of agony. Have you not noticed that those who have time for you are those who have endured sufferings? All others are too busily engaged in selfish endeavors to stop and help the weary travelers. You are not to be among the too-busy.

When you have received your comfort and consolation

96

from me, you will share in the sorrow and the comfort of others.

"See, I have refined you, though not as silver; I have tested you in the furnace of affliction. For my own sake...I do this" (Isaiah 48:10,11).

△ △ △

Thorny Path

Lord, *what else do You have to say to me regarding the thorny path You are leading me through?*

My Child, when you dedicated your life to me, I accepted your offering. You chose to do my will. But in choosing my will you unwittingly chose a path which, for a time, is hedged about with thorns.

In the eyes of the world you are in a terrible place. Many who do not understand me believe you to be where you are because of your own folly. But I have placed you where you are for my glory. I will be glorified because my will is being fulfilled in you.

I desire you to maintain with Habakkuk, "The Sovereign Lord is my strength; he makes my feet like the feet of a deer, he enables me to go on the heights" (Habakkuk 3:19). When you have become victorious on the lowlands, I indeed will lead you to the heights. I delight in leading my children to high places, but first, much must be learned in the valleys.

It is in the valleys that you are learning to desire me for myself and not for anything you might obtain through me. After you have drunk the cup I handed you in the valley, you will find that its contents have become sweet within you. Then you will be strengthened to ascend to the heights.

Groping

Lord, *I know You are the Light of the world, but it seems I'm still groping in darkness. Where is the light?*

My Child, the light is within you even though you are not aware of it.

Remember when I gave Moses instructions for building the tabernacle? I told him to keep the lamps burning from evening until morning. The Israelites brought clear oil of pressed olives for the lamps. The lamps burned in the tabernacle every night as a statute throughout the generations.

The tabernacle represented my presence with the Israelites. But now you are my living tabernacle, and my lamp burns within you. As the light shining in the old tabernacle obliterating the darkness, so I, the Light of the world, dwell within you to obliterate your darkness. Your pressures surrendered to me and blessed by the Holy Spirit enhance the oil in your lamp.

Do not look outside yourself for the light. You are my child and of my kingdom. My kingdom is a kingdom of light. You have been looking at circumstances, but my light within you empowers you to see beyond all present appearances.

"Arise, shine, for your light has come, and the glory of the Lord rises upon you" (Isaiah 60:1).

Isolation

Lord, *I feel cut off from life, like I'm on the outside looking in. Why such pain?*

My Child, you feel crushed because of yesterday's hurts, your dreams that did not come true. You must turn your back on all the hurts of your past. "Remember not the former things, neither consider the things of old. Behold, I will do a new thing.... I will even make a way in the wilderness, and rivers in the desert" (Isaiah 43:18,19 KJV).

Put behind you those hopes and plans that failed. Refuse to entertain the rejection thoughts that are crowding into your mind. Replace all negative thinking with the glad assurance that you are accepted by me. Then you will be led out of your wilderness of frustration into the fertile valley of joy.

Your experiences have given you a sense of unimportance and inferiority. Regardless of how you feel about yourself, you are important to me and to my kingdom here on earth.

You are not alone. Neither are you on the outside. I am making your life all you ever desired it to be, all I have planned for you. Trust my grace to lead you into the fulfillment you desire.

"You will go out in joy and be led forth in peace" (Isaiah 55:12).

Abandonment Through Trials

Lord, *what supreme lesson am I to learn through the circumstances I find myself in?*

My Child, you do well to ask "What am I to learn?" and not merely "Why?" You have learned not to question why I work as I do.

You are learning total abandonment to me. I want all my children to learn what I am teaching you (and many will learn from you)—to trust me completely.

Abandonment is to give up any selfish claim on your life, to surrender to my mercy yourself and everything pertaining to your life. Only those who know that I am truly love and compassion are able to surrender themselves to me.

Trials serve to teach you your own insufficiency apart from me. When the prodigal son came to the end of himself, he returned to his father. You have not been a prodigal, but you did need to come to the end of your own resources in order to realize that I, and I alone, can satisfy. I alone can fulfill your needs—spiritual, emotional, physical, and financial. I am your source, and through me you can do all things. Apart from me you can do nothing.

"The Lord is the strength of his people, a fortress of salvation for his anointed one" (Psalm 28:8).

Relinquishment

Lord, *is there something else You have to say to me about relinquishment?*

My Child, it is only after relinquishment of your selfish ambitions that you can realize union with me. This is what Paul calls the life that "is hidden with Christ in God" (Colossians 3:3).

Children of this world are afraid to let go of selfish desires. They do not understand that my desires for them are higher than their own. If they would exchange their self-assertiveness apart from me to a self-confidence which comes from a Christ-consciousness, all their desires could be fulfilled.

My promise in Proverbs 16:3 applies here: "Commit to the Lord whatever you do, and your plans will succeed." To commit to me whatever you do is to roll it over on me, not concerning yourself with it, but knowing that anything relinquished to me is bound to succeed.

Relinquishment does not mean quitting or passive resignation. It does mean surrendering the struggle to my hands, handing over to me every detail of your life. The more you let go, the more my grace abounds to you. The way of spiritual progress is relinquishment—exchanging your inadequate self for my all-powerful self.

"Taste and see that the Lord is good; blessed is the man who takes refuge in him" (Psalm 34:8).

Fatigue

Lord, *my body is so tired. Even after a night of sleep, I feel exhausted. Is there no rest for me during this trial?*

My Child, fatigue nearly always accompanies a heavy heart. "A crushed spirit dries up the bones" (Proverbs 17:22b). Your body cannot escape being affected by your crushed spirit.

But a "cheerful heart has a continual feast" and is "good medicine" (Proverbs 15:15; 17:22a). The key to turning your weakness into strength is to praise me. Praise can transform your heavy heart into a cheerful heart.

Your only hope of survival is in praise. Praise will bring refreshment to your soul and body. Force yourself to praise me. Look to me in the joyful confidence that I will lead you into green pastures and beside still waters.

I am your Shepherd. Praise me for who I am, and you will be revitalized in spirit and body. Joy and praise are healing. I came to give you abundant life. It is yours. Abundance of joy and strength are available to you as you lift your soul in adoration to me. Morning will come, and with it sunrise in your soul. You will know that my Spirit has pervaded your spirit.

"You who fear the Lord, praise him" (Psalm 22:23).

Profit from Darkness

Lord, *I don't want anything which comes to me to be wasted. Show me how to let these dark times be profitable in Your kingdom.*

My Child, be assured that I waste nothing. As you yield yourself and your circumstances to me, the things happening to you will be useful to you and to me. Only be sure that you do not feel crushed but *served* by every situation. As Glenn Clark said, "Trouble is actually one of the greatest blessings that can come to a man . . . provided he knows how to use it and not let it use him."

To worry about a situation is to ascribe more power to the situation than to me. Without realizing it, most individuals are doing just that. Remember that just as surely as I stilled the tempest in the night on the sea of Galilee, I can still the tempest in the night of your sea of trouble.

Neither my power nor my love has ever lessened. As you immerse yourself in my love, letting me become more and more real to you, this time of trouble will be profitable not only to you but also to others whom I will later send to you for comfort.

Keep yourself free from envy and jealousy. Live in a state of continual forgiveness. See that neither fear nor distrust blur your vision of me, and you can be sure of receiving your request.

"I will give you the treasures of darkness, riches stored in secret places, so that you may know that I am the Lord" (Isaiah 45:3).

❧ ❧ ❧

Rejoice at All Times

Lord, *I know Your Word teaches that we are to rejoice at all times. How can I do it in a time like this?*

My Child, the secret to rejoicing at all times is in knowing that I know the outcome. My purposes prevail and my purposes are always good. So find ways to praise me in the midst of your trial. The book of Psalms is full of praises to help you in your worship and praise. Imitate David's praises.

You cannot praise and rejoice as long as your eyes are on your circumstances. Look above and beyond your circumstances to my face. I am your comfort; I am your health; I am your courage and strength. Meditate on the truth of my all-sufficiency and rejoice in that.

I am to you what rain is to the desert, what the sun is to growing plants, what the sky is to eagles, what air is to every living creature. I am your life, your joy-giver. Drink freely of my love and be refreshed. My love is as a stream of living water that can never be diminished.

The day is coming when this water will be bubbling up in you as a river of joy to those whom I will send to you. Believe and rejoice, knowing that I have spoken the truth to you today.

"Let all who take refuge in you be glad; let them ever sing for joy" (Psalm 5:11).

Pain of Loss

Lord, *I didn't want to lose what seemingly I have lost. How can the pain of loss be alleviated?*

My Child, nothing of lasting value lies within your own power of accomplishment, but all things are possible with me. You read correctly when you read, "The disciple is a disciple only insofar as he shares his Lord's suffering and rejection and crucifixion." Rejoice that you are a disciple.

To deny self is to become more aware of me than of yourself. The more you learn to keep your eyes on me rather than on your stony path, the less you'll feel the pain.

I have prepared the way for you. If I had not, you would find the road unbearable. Every Christian has his own peculiar cross, but only those who are dead to their own selfish desires are able to bear up under their crosses.

Those who live in constant communion with me become less and less aware of the pain. Suffering is overcome by suffering. Rest in the assurance that you are growing in your understanding, and that your pain gradually is becoming less acute.

"Know that the Lord has set apart the godly for himself" (Psalm 4:3a).

No Awareness of His Presence

Lord, *the hurts continue to pile up. My moments of feeling Your peace are so few. I struggle in vain to be aware of Your presence in the midst of this turmoil.*

My Child, all struggling must cease before you can be aware of me. Awareness of my presence comes from resting in me. Do you not remember the words I spoke to you in the night last week? "The battle is not yours, but mine." And after that I reminded you that "he that dwelleth in the secret place of the Most High shall abide under the shadow of the Almighty" (Psalm 91:1 KJV).

A few days later I spoke to you through my servant, confirming those words: "From the shadow of my wing know that the battle is not yours but mine. And from the shadow of my wing stand still and see the salvation of the Lord."

I know your hurts are real. I have not turned a deaf ear to the harsh things spoken against you, nor have I been blind to the rejection you are suffering. I am allowing these things only because they are a necessary part of your preparation for a larger service in my kingdom.

Realize that you are to look only to me for your joy. Seek not for it in the actions or words of others. You will not find it there. In my own time I will deliver you. Meanwhile look to me in complete faith that I am in charge.

Ominous Clouds

Lord, as I review my recent past, I recall many more clouds than sunshine. And now these clouds have become so dark and ominous that I see little hope for my future.

My Child, do you not know that in the Bible clouds are often an evidence of my presence and that I make the clouds my chariots? I have not changed.

When Moses went up on Mount Sinai to receive the covenant, my glory settled over the mountain and I spoke to Moses from the cloud. Later, when the Israelites set up a tabernacle for a meeting place, my glory filled the tabernacle. "Moses could not enter the Tent of Meeting because the cloud had settled upon it, and the glory of the Lord filled the tabernacle" (Exodus 40:35).

In all the travels of the Israelites, I guided them with my cloud. By night a fire was in the cloud to give my people light and guidance.

You are to understand by faith that the clouds in your life are for your ultimate good. At present you are unaware of the warm fire within the clouds around you, but it is there. That fire contained in your cloud is not only providing you with enough light to keep you on the path I have chosen for you, but it is also purifying you for a service you cannot yet understand.

So rest in the knowledge that I am with you, even in the clouds.

"He makes the clouds his chariot and rides on the wings of the wind" (Psalm 104:3).

❧ ❧ ❧

Perplexities Within and Without

Lord, *I feel crushed by the pressures from within and without. I believe I could handle the outside perplexities if I were not so bewildered by those within.*

My Child, you are feeling what all my set-apart ones feel when they yield themselves to the refiner's fire. But I will not allow you to be crushed by any weight put upon you. "God is faithful; he will not let you be tempted beyond what you can bear. But when you are tempted, he will also provide a way out so that you can stand up under it" (1 Corinthians 10:13).

You are correct in your belief that you could handle the outside perplexities *if.* It's the outside problems that are meant to bring you into an undisturbed relationship with me. When you have grown to the place of a more conscious awareness of my presence within you, you will hardly notice such outside events as those disturbing you now.

When my servant Stephen was being stoned to death, he "looked up to heaven and saw the glory of God, and Jesus standing at the right hand of God. . . . Then he fell on his knees and cried out, 'Lord, do not hold this sin against them' " (Acts 7:55,60).

The day is close at hand when you joyfully will forgive

those who are hurting you. Your concern will be only for their welfare. My Holy Spirit within you will bring this about. Rejoice in me while you expectantly wait for that day.

Light in the Darkness

Lord, *I don't want to give in to my feelings and revel in my darkness. I am aware that I could carve out a rut of self-pity and abide there. How can I be sure of avoiding such error?*

My Child, you are on the right course. You have faced rather than resisted your darkness. You have confessed your need and accepted my love. In so doing you have avoided compounding darkness with guilt. You have been adopted into my kingdom. That makes you a special person having no need for self-pity. All your needs are met because of who I am.

No life is exempt from times of darkness. When darkness is accepted as a natural part of living, discouragement can be warded off. The Christian life is one which can recognize that the dark valley is not eternal. When the end is reached, light dawns again.

When you felt I was a million miles away and that your faith counted for nothing, even when you almost despaired of life itself, you dared affirm one thing which kept you believing that light would finally dawn: "All things are working together for good." That sustained you. Continue now in the path you have chosen.

"Even in darkness light dawns for the upright" (Psalm 112:4).

Ill Advice

Lord, *this battle would be much easier if my friends were more loving toward my offenders. I am beginning to see Your hand of goodness in my circumstances, but how do I handle those who offer well-meaning advice contrary to my convictions?*

My Child, deep within your heart you know the answer to your question. But you have been programmed to be a people-pleaser. Since one you loved turned aside from you, you quite naturally want to respond favorably in the eyes of your friends.

But some of my children respond poorly to crises. A few are counseling you to use worldly wisdom and "common sense." I have chosen you to risk all on the basis of my teaching. You have the power to turn a polite but deaf ear to any advice not in perfect alignment with my Word. Your only obligation is to me. When you please me, I will take care of all else for you.

I have put my wisdom within your heart. "Do not forsake wisdom, and she will protect you" (Proverbs 4:6). Let my wisdom dictate your treatment of your advisors. Love and pray for them that they may "understand the fear of the Lord and find the knowledge of God" (Proverbs 2:5).

Tested Faith

Lord, *I know Your Word emphasizes the necessity of having absolute faith in You. This trial is thoroughly testing my faith. I want to believe this episode will end in good, as You promise, but it's still sometimes hard.*

My Child, humanity cannot see as I see. You would like to know how your present circumstances will end. Only I know the future. But you can trust your future to my hands.

You must allow your faith to develop. Overcome your doubts and fears by eliminating distrustful thinking from your mind. Let positive, constructive thoughts continually fill your mind.

Let my words which you have memorized wash your mind clean. Over and over quote the Scripture promises until they become a part of your very nature. Every time you catch yourself thinking a gloomy thought, reverse the gears of your mind. Replace the unwanted thought with uplifting reflections of my goodness.

Your resolve to be victorious is evidence of faith that you can be. Your faith is gradually enlarged as you make my words the meditation of your heart day and night. "Faith is being sure of what we hope for and certain of what we do not see" (Hebrews 11:1). Do all within your power to remain composed while you wait for the fulfillment of my promise to reward you.

Security in Surrender

Lord, I heard one of Your servants say, "When you chose to follow Jesus, you voluntarily surrendered the right to choose the circumstances or the power to vary the consequences of your decision." I have chosen to follow You. Is what I am experiencing part of the cost of discipleship?

Yes, My Child, and when you were told that "the disciple is dragged out of his relative security into a life of absolute insecurity," you were told the truth then too. But what the world calls insecurity is absolute security and safety of fellowship with me. To rely on me is to choose the only real security. You are moving out of the realm of finite into the infinite. You are breaking through past sets of laws into the realization that nothing has any ultimate significance except my life in you.

Your experiences are teaching you that there is neither life nor discipleship in abstract Christianity and religious knowledge. My life to be lived through you requires that all ties with the world be broken so you may commit yourself fully to the incarnate Son of God.

Inasmuch as you have chosen to surrender your will to mine, you may ask and expect my power to enable you to obtain the spiritual victory you desire. "Commit your way to the Lord; trust in him and he will do this" (Psalm 37:5).

Enriched Through Darkness

Lord, *I know that through You we have victory. Are there individuals who actually live above periods of darkness?*

My Child, those who claim to never feel any shrouds of darkness are the ones who have never taken time to be still. Their busy lives keep them on the move so that turning inward is unknown to them. Without realizing it, these individuals are trapped in a somewhat shallow, meaningless existence. But when tragedy strikes, they find themselves severely handicapped, unable to take it.

Living life fully requires times of darkness. How else could you have known your own weakness and your need of me? How else could you have known the depths of your own being? Without passing through your darkness, could you have known the reality of my having conquered death and darkness? No, you would have known it intellectually, but now you know it experientially. Now when other periods of gloom come, you will be able to look beyond the shadows to the One who conquered all.

You will know beyond intellectual understanding that my grace is sufficient. You will be comforted in the assurance that I can and will untangle the twisted threads in the web of your life. You will know as David knew: "It was good for me to be afflicted so that I might learn your decrees" (Psalm 119:71).

Wounds in the Deep Mind

Lord, *I realize from what You've taught me that many of my hurts are deep in my subconscious mind. Can I ever be rid of them?*

My Child, your desire to be cleansed of your deep-seated hurts is the first step toward wholeness. Just as you exercised your will to forgive those who wronged you, and gradually the feeling of forgiveness came, so it is with repressed hurts. Indeed, you laid the foundation for your own healing on the day you totally forgave your offenders. You are on the path to wholeness.

Restoring the inner being is a process requiring patience and persistence on your part. You must "cultivate, carry out to the goal and fully complete your own salvation with reverence and awe and trembling...for it is God Who is all the while effectually at work in you... both to will and to work for His good pleasure and satisfaction and delight" (Philippians 2:12,13 AMP).

Your part in the process is to cooperate with me. Replace all condemnatory thoughts about yourself, your past, and other people with positive thoughts. Although you cannot control your subconscious mind, you can voluntarily feed it constructive, healthy truths. You have complete control over the matter that reaches your deep mind. Your dominant thoughts impress your heart and influence your whole being. "A happy heart is a good medicine and a cheerful mind works healing" (Proverbs 17:22 AMP).

Cultivate the habit of meditating on my love. Daily read my promises. Know that I am able to do immeasurably more than all you ask or imagine, according to my power that is at work within you. My power *is* at work within you. Believe it. You *are* being relieved of every hurt.

🖋 🖋 🖋

Peace Seems Elusive

Lord, *peace seems to be such an elusive ele-ment. I strive for it and think I have it, but then it's gone again.*

My Child, lasting peace is not a thing sepa-rated from me. I am the God of peace, as Paul wrote: "Live in peace, and the God of love and peace will be with you" (2 Corinthians 13:11). You shut yourself off from peace by striving for it. As the God of peace, it is my purpose to give you peace.

"Do not fret or have any anxiety about anything. . . . And God's peace . . . which transcends all understanding, shall garrison and mount guard over your hearts and minds in Christ Jesus" (Philippians 4:6,7 AMP). Your *anxiety* about your lack of peace intensifies your problem of receiving my peace.

Rest in the assurance that having me, you have my peace. You did not earn a place in my kingdom. Neither do you earn peace. It is my free gift to you. The peace I give you is not the peace the world gives. The world's peace depends upon circumstances and is fleeting. Just as I am eternal, so is my peace.

Stop examining yourself. Simply rest in me as an infant rests in its mother's arms. Rejoice in me. Do not be afraid of making a mistake. Because you have committed your life to me, you can trust that I am leading you in all your decisions.

"Let the peace...from the Christ rule...in your hearts" (Colossians 3:15 AMP).

❧ ❧ ❧

Finding Life

Lord, *You seem to be saying that those who are to have a place in Your service must first have a place of suffering. So right now I'm underlining these words: "If any man will come after me, let him deny himself, and take up his cross daily, and follow me. For whosoever will save his life shall lose it, but whosoever will lose his life for my sake, the same shall save it" (Luke 9:23,24 KJV).*

Until now I've shied away from these words. I know it will cost me more than I realize, but I choose to follow You, whatever the cost. If it means being misunderstood, if it means continued separation from someone or something I hold dear, let it be. Only let me feel Your presence.

My Child, your months of intense emotional suffering have brought you to the place I had planned for you. Yes, the way is costly, but the rewards are great. I correct and discipline everyone I love. Submit to my discipline and know that I'm dealing with you as my beloved Child. "For the time being no discipline brings joy but seems grievous and painful, but afterwards it yields the peaceable fruit of righteousness" (Hebrews 12:11 AMP).

Wait for me and I will reveal myself to you. I am honored by your waiting and trusting. Patient waiting brings a rich reward. There will be times when you cannot feel my nearness. These are the times to trust me without feeling. Remember that I am with you always.

♔ ♔ ♔

Part Two

Into His Glorious Light!

Emerging from the Tunnel

Lord, *I realize I cannot change my past. I have given to You my misdeeds along with my pains and disappointments. With Your divine life in me, I have forgiven myself and those who failed me. I am not only comforted but made joyful by Your love. I choose only to please You. What would You have me do?*

My Child, as you continue regular periods of stillness in my presence and with my written Word, you soon will find emerging from the depths of your heart a desire that I planted there in your childhood.

All that has transpired in your life was necessary preparation for the larger work I have designed for you. When that desire begins to surface, recognize that it is from me. When I said, "Delight yourself in the Lord and he will give you the desires of your heart," I meant not only that I will grant your heart's desires, but that I will put within your heart the desires which spring forth into your mind.

Listen to the voice of that desire when it makes itself known to you. Cultivate it and you will be completely fulfilled because you will be accomplishing my purpose for you.

"The Lord is righteous in all his ways and loving toward all he has made. The Lord is near to all who call on him.... He fulfills the desires of those who fear him" (Psalm 145:17-19).

A Clean Slate

Lord, *I thank You that You have forgiven me of all my little mistakes and confusion as well as my big sins. And I'm almost as grateful that I've been able to forgive myself and others. It's a good feeling to have the slate wiped clean. You have given me a life filled with peace and joy. Your life and love within me provide both power and tranquility.*

"I will praise you, O Lord, among the nations; I will sing of you among the peoples. For great is your love, higher than the heavens; your faithfulness reaches to the skies" (Psalm 108:3,4).

My Child, as the all-wise and all-loving God that I am, I desire only the highest of everything for my children. Nothing is too insignificant for my care. I am deeply interested in everything that concerns you. My love prompted me to provide a complete salvation for you. Absolutely nothing is outside the realm of my magnificent provision. There is always hope and help.

"Light is shed upon the righteous and joy on the upright in heart. Rejoice in the Lord, you who are righteous" (Psalm 97:11,12).

Delighting in His Steadfastness

Lord, *I just want to thank You for Your faithfulness to me. Paul truly expressed Your steadfastness when he said of You, "If we are faithless, he will remain faithful" (2 Timothy 2:13).*

I believe I'm catching a glimpse of what the prophet Habakkuk saw. He was so certain of your steadfastness that he declared that if all his crops failed to produce, he would still rejoice in you. If under the Old Covenant Habakkuk could be joyful in you, how much more I who live under the New Covenant! I am able to follow Paul's instructions to "sing and make music in your heart to the Lord" (Ephesians 5:19) because of Your joy bubbling up within me.

My Child, because you have chosen to delight in me, you are finding a personal fulfillment of Isaiah's prophecy: "The Lord will guide you always; he will satisfy your needs in a sun-scorched land and will strengthen your frame. You will be like a well-watered garden, like a spring whose waters never fail" (Isaiah 58:11).

Be assured that regardless of any calamity, my eyes are continually upon my children. I delight in supplying all your needs. The immeasurable bounties in my storehouse are exceeded only by my pleasure in lavishing good things upon my children.

Rejoicing in Him

Lord, I thank You for the experiences You have chosen for me. There were many I would not have chosen, but You knew the lessons I needed to learn through them and the joy which would result. I know now, as I otherwise could not have comprehended, that my fulfillment and joy come only from You.

You have shown me that joy depends not on external stimuli, but from realizing that You live within me, empowering me to be triumphant in all circumstances. How grateful I am to be assured of Your same faithfulness that released the psalmist David to soar above situations which could have imprisoned him in caves of despair!

Now I am free to exult with the apostle Paul, "Oh, the depth of the riches of the wisdom and knowledge of God! For from him and through him and to him are all things. . . . Rejoice in the Lord always" (Romans 11:33,36; Philippians 4:4).

My Child, as you grow in your awareness of my delight in you, you will be released to be even more joyful in me. Before the creation of the world I chose you and lavished upon you the riches of my grace. Indeed, I work out everything in conformity with my purposes, and my purposes always abound with good for those who choose to follow me.

I would remind you of the words of my apostle concerning my love for you: "I pray also that the eyes of your heart may be enlightened in order that you may know the hope to which he has called you, the riches of his glorious inheritance in the saints, and his incomparably great power for us who believe" (Ephesians 1:18,19).

Rejoice in knowing that not only do you have an inheritance in me, but I have **an** inheritance in you.

৯ ৯ ৯

A New Song

Lord, *when I was sinking in the mire of self-rejection, You lifted me up. I am grateful to be able to say with the psalmist, "He lifted me out of the slimy pit, out of the mud and mire; he set my feet on a rock and gave me a firm place to stand. He put a new song in my mouth, a hymn of praise to our God" (Psalm 40:2,3).*

Because of Your love, I am revived and I look joyfully to the future. I will not look back, but ahead. You have given me a new dream, a dream that I know I can see fulfilled with Your help. I will use the abilities you have given me to accomplish a higher goal than I formerly thought possible. I have chosen my goal. At last I realize that You have not planned for my life to be a failure but a success. I trust You to open and close doors, and I will respond.

My Child, you have tapped the spring of my joy. Hold your vision in spite of inevitable obstacles and you will find the joy to be a bubbling stream. Never forget the availability of my power. "Those who hope in the Lord will renew their strength. They will soar on wings like eagles; they will run and not be weary, they will walk and not be faint" (Isaiah 40:31).

Fulfilled in Him

Lord, *my experiences have proved to me that joy is as readily born of difficulty as of ease. I am grateful for the sure hope born within me when You showed me I could decide to make the best of a situation over which I had no control.*

You taught me that I could be joyous in You regardless of what happened to me. I have learned that I can be fulfilled in You, and in You alone. When I surrendered my will to Yours I discovered a power beyond myself. For that gift I am most appreciative.

My Child, you made a giant step forward the day you chose to accept the right attitude toward yourself and your situation. You determined to believe me when I assured you I would work all things out for your good. You exercised your will to believe you were somebody when your circumstances were screaming that you were nobody.

You elected to believe my promise: "Never will I leave you; never will I forsake you" (Hebrews 13:5). When a few misguided friends offered you ill advice, you chose to immerse yourself in my written Word and to follow such instructions as, "Make every effort to live in peace .... See...that no bitter root grows up to cause trouble" (Hebrews 12:14,15).

You made every effort to believe the words I spoke

133

through James: "Consider it pure joy...whenever you face trials of many kinds, because you know that the testing of your faith develops perseverance" (James 1:2).

❧ ❧ ❧

Free to Be Myself

Lord, *I thank You that out of my recent experiences has come the understanding that I am free to be myself—joyfully. I don't have to be a carbon copy of anybody else. I am the unique expression of Your creativity.*

You have shown me that as the sun shines through stained-glass windows, casting its hues according to the color of the windowpanes, so your love is expressed through the unique person that I am. Today I rejoice in the realization that I don't have to struggle to make myself a worthy channel. I am privileged to yield myself to You as the violin yields its strings to its master's touch.

My Child, I'm glad you are discovering that I enjoy variety in my flower garden. How sad I would be if the buttercups tried to be roses or if the daffodils tried to make themselves into tulips. I delight in every plant that blooms. You are part of my planting.

Would you want your children to be just alike? Are you not gladdened by their differences? Neither do you compare their strengths and weaknesses. You love and accept each one in his or her present stage of development. How much more do I for each of my children!

Continue to rejoice in your own individuality. I live within you to express myself through you individually in all places and at all times for the glory of my name. Joyously celebrate life with this understanding.

"Sing praises to the Lord, enthroned in Zion; proclaim among the nations what he has done" (Psalm 9:11).

❧ ❧ ❧

Enjoying My Uniqueness

Lord, again I come to thank You for the freedom I have in knowing that You accept me as I am. I'm glad I don't have to conform to any image but Yours. So many voices in the world used to confuse me. I wondered who I was. Now I know.

I thank You for the freedom You have given me to be me and to grow at my own speed. I'm glad You won't cast me aside or even become impatient with me if I fail to progress as rapidly today as I did yesterday.

"Your love, O Lord, reaches to the heavens, your faithfulness to the skies" (Psalm 36:5).

My Child, you are learning that the goal which matters is your union with me. When your aim is to exalt me, you are free to follow your own inclinations. Rooted in my love, your desires coincide with my desires.

My life is expressed in each child of mine as each yields himself to me. Each expression of my being is different, just as each snowflake is different. Even though you may be doing the same work as thousands of others, your work will be distinct because it is expressed through a unique channel. I make it so.

Remember that I have planted my desires within your heart. Be still and listen to me, and you will ascertain more fully what those desires are. Remember too that I will maintain my love to you forever, and that my covenant with you will never fail (Psalm 89:28). Therefore I remind you: "Rejoice in the Lord always. I will say it again: Rejoice!" (Philippians 4:4).

❧ ❧ ❧

A New Creation

Lord, *my heart overflows with gratitude for the new joy You have given me. My deepened understanding that I am a new creation in Christ adds zest to my life. How well Paul spoke when he stated, "The old has gone, the new has come!" (2 Corinthians 5:17).*

You were not impatient with my tortoiselike pace in grasping the concept that Your kingdom is "righteousness, peace and joy in the Holy Spirit" (Romans 14:17). Your righteousness imparted to me has etched indescribable joy on my innermost being. I am content. No longer bound by circumstances, my heart takes wings. I am established in Your love.

I join the psalmist in saying, "Therefore I will praise you among the nations, O Lord; I will sing praise to your name" (Psalm 18:49).

My Child, I rejoice that you have entered into a new measure of joy. You are learning that there is victory in praise itself. One who has learned to praise me in all things has discovered how to transcend much that would be defeating without the ingredient of praise.

My children walk in greater freedom when they understand that I inspired the psalmist with more than mere words as he wrote:

Shout for joy to the Lord, all the earth,
burst into jubilant song with music;
make music to the Lord with the harp,
with the harp and the sound of singing,
with trumpets and the blast of the ram's horn—
shout for joy before the Lord, the King (Psalm 98:4-6).

Choosing Abundant Life

Lord, *for a long time I sought to change persons and situations. I thought that would solve all my problems. I am grateful that You showed me that all change must begin from within. You made clear to me that You have given me the power to choose abundant life. I don't have to be bound by past circumstances. I need only change my attitude.*

Thanks to You, Lord, I have "put on the new self, which is being renewed in the image of its Creator" (Colossians 3:10). How good it is to know I am a new creation in Christ! I don't have to conform any longer to the pattern of this world, but I can continually be transformed by the renewing of my mind (Romans 12:2).

My Child, you have learned what it means to "Be joyful in hope, patient in affliction, faithful in prayer" (Romans 12:12). Furthermore, you have learned to bless those who persecute you and to live in harmony with yourself and others (Romans 12:14,16). This is the road to victory.

"Whether you turn to the right or to the left, your ears will hear a voice behind you, saying, 'This is the way; walk in it' " (Isaiah 30:21). Keep going.

Set Apart to God

Lord, *today when I read in the book of Kings about the dedication of the temple, I was especially impressed with Solomon's dedicatory prayer. He reminded me that You singled Israel out from all the nations of the world to be your own inheritance (1 Kings 8:53). Those people lived under the Old Covenant. How much more am I (of the New Covenant) singled out to be Your inheritance. How blessed I am!*

After the temple was dedicated, the people went home "joyful and glad in heart for all the good" You had done. How much more reason I have to be joyful for all the good You have done and are doing! The thrill of knowing I am Your purchased possession causes me to sing with the psalmist, "Praise the Lord! For the Lord is good; sing praises to His name, for that is pleasant. For the Lord has chosen [me] for Himself. . .for His peculiar possession and treasure" (Psalm 135:3,4 AMP).

My Child, as I esteemed the prayer of Solomon that day, I also honor your prayer. It was I who consecrated the temple of Jerusalem "by putting my name there forever." In like manner, I have consecrated you and set you apart for myself. My name is stamped upon your heart as a reminder to you of my abiding presence.

I reside within you that you may be filled with joy in all you do.

I have come that you may have life, and have it to the full (John 10:10). Be filled with gladness. Let your whole being radiate my joy.

❧ ❧ ❧

Putting Off and
Putting On

Lord, Lord, I've been noticing how often Your Word admonishes us to "put off" and "put on." You've given us so many helps for victorious living. I'm glad Your Holy Spirit inspired Paul to write, "Put off your old self. . .put on the new self" (Ephesians 4:22-24). This means You have given me the ability to do the putting off and putting on.

What a joy to know that I can "put off and discard [my] old unrenewed self—which characterized [my] previous manner of life. . .and be constantly renewed in the spirit of [my] mind—having a fresh mental and spiritual attitude" (Ephesians 4:22,23 AMP).

It seems that when I make the choice to say goodbye to my old defeated way of looking at life and accept Your triumphant way, the putting off and putting on come almost automatically. Thank You, Lord, that through You our problems have to go.

My Child, you are discovering the keys. They are all revealed in my Word. "So I say to you, Ask and keep on asking, and it shall be given you; seek and keep on seeking, and you shall find; knock and keep on knocking, and the door shall be opened to you" (Luke 11:9 AMP).

Yes, the first key is "Choice." "I have set before you life and death, blessings and curses. Now choose life"

144

(Deuteronomy 30:19). These words which I gave to the early Israelites are just as applicable to you.

You have chosen life and blessings, and by that choice you chose to put off everything destructive and put on a seeking attitude, opening the door to my treasure house of bounty.

🕊 🕊 🕊

Abiding in Christ

Lord, how truly Andrew Murray stated, "Abiding fully in Christ is a life of exquisite and overflowing happiness." Your joy has become mine. Lord, I thank You for the divine exchange you made on the cross. You took my griefs and pains that I might have Your joy and health. Let me never forget it. The joy of heaven has become mine now in full measure. Because of Your joy in me, I am victorious over every adversity.

"I will extol the Lord at all times; his praise will always be on my lips. My soul will boast in the Lord; let the afflicted hear and rejoice" (Psalm 34:1,2).

My Child, I am delighted with your response to my truth. Nothing pleases me more than for my children to discover the realities hidden in me and in my Word. When my sons and daughters know that truth sets them free, they no longer strain at life. They let my life flow through theirs, freely and joyously.

You were called to be free, not to be ensnared by a yoke of bondage. I came that you might be completely liberated. As you stand firm in the liberty I purchased for you, responsive to my Spirit, joy will continually accompany you. "The fruit of the (Holy) Spirit . . . is love, joy . . . peace, patience" (Galatians 5:22 AMP).

A Living Hope

Lord, I thank You for Your patience in teaching me the meaning of faith and hope. I realize I am learning only slowly to trust You completely. Your bearing with me sustains my hope.

I am inspired by the example of Abraham. Even though human reason for hope was gone, he hoped on in faith (Romans 4:18 AMP). He had no child, and he and his wife, Sarah, were well past the age of becoming parents when You assured him that his offspring would be as numerous as the stars. He believed You, and You credited his belief to his account as righteousness.

My human nature too often demands evidence before moving in faith and hope, but Your Word tells me that "hope that is seen is no hope at all" (Romans 8:24). Again You remind me that I am to be not only "joyful in hope" but also "patient in affliction, faithful in prayer" (Romans 12:12).

So today I reaffirm Your indwelling presence and yield myself to You to be hope within me. I choose to hope in You and to be a channel of hope to others.

My Child, just as my Spirit inspired Peter to write, so I remind you now: In my great mercy I have given you new birth into a living hope (1 Peter 1:3). This living hope abides in you to help you become all you desire to be for my glory. With my help you can handle or change situations. Hope propels you beyond doubt into faith, which enables you to answer affirmatively the question I asked Abraham: "Is anything too hard for the Lord?" (Genesis 18:14).

☙ ☙ ☙

A Sharer of His Nature

Lord, Your Word continually unfolds new and fresh revelations of old truths. I thank You for the power of Your Holy Spirit to illuminate and show me the meanings I've missed.

One passage which has become especially meaningful to me is 2 Peter 1:3,4: "His divine power has given us everything we need for life and godliness through our knowledge of him who called us by his own glory and goodness. Through these he has given us his very great and precious promises, so that through them you may participate in the divine nature."

How awesome to realize that You have already made total provision for us—everything we'll ever need for life and godliness! The promises are all dependent upon our personal knowledge of You. What a tremendous concept for my finite mind to grasp! It's up to me to move into a fuller knowledge of You. I choose to accept the challenge.

My Child, indeed layer upon layer of truth is contained in my Word. Because of my unfathomable love I have made it so.

My apostle John expressed it well: "How great is the love the Father has lavished on us, that we should be called children of God! And that is what we are!"

(1 John 3:1). Since you are my child, then all things are yours. You are more than you realize and you have more than you are aware of. Discover, believe, and receive.

❧ ❧ ❧

Pleasure in Him

Lord, I am rejoicing in the knowledge that You desire to reveal Yourself to me. It is exciting to know that the Creator of the universe loves and trusts me enough to declare, "The Lord confides in those who fear him; he makes his covenant known to them" (Psalm 25:14). What a challenge to me to reverence You more completely! How can I do other than hope and trust in Him who is the Light of my life?

How accurately Jeanne Guyon expressed my thoughts when she wrote, "Once you have tasted the sweetness of His love, you will find that your selfish desires no longer hold power. You will find it impossible to have pleasure in anything except Him. . . . All the Lord's children have been called to the enjoyment of God—an enjoyment that can be known both in this life as well as in the life to come." Such awareness releases within me new energies to keep moving onward and motivates me to add up my assets. Because of Your indwelling presence and power, I am setting new goals for myself and advancing in enthusiasm.

My Child, you are uncovering the truth that "the law of the Lord is perfect, reviving the soul" (Psalm 19:7). Your recognition of my perfect way indeed propels you into the more abundant life I have planned for you. To the faithful I show myself faithful. You are on your way.

A New Vitality

Lord, how perfectly the psalmist expressed the truth of my heart when he said, "You have given me hope" (Psalm 119:49). Your love has made me know that You consider me an important person. You know all there is to know about me, and You still love me beyond measure. You have given my life completeness.

Because of You, Lord, there is within me a rising tide of spiritual awareness and power. With my life centered in You, every day abounds with vitality. I am able to transcend everyday circumstances that might spell gloom, and I abound in Your radiance.

I am experiencing what Paul proclaimed: "Where the Spirit of the Lord is, there is freedom. And we, who with unveiled faces all reflect the Lord's glory, are being transformed into his likeness with ever-increasing glory" (2 Corinthians 3:17,18).

My Child, the more you learn to practice living with joyous vitality, the more you will find an increase of this gladsome power. Training yourself to be aware of my loving presence accomplishes wonders that nothing else can accomplish. Let my kingdom within you shine forth to promote abundant living. Pursuing me above all else pays off dividends of joy.

"Blessed is he whose help is the God of Jacob, whose hope is in the Lord his God" (Psalm 146:5).

Reflecting His Glory

Lord, *I recently read that life's greatest achievement is becoming remade by Yourself so that we know how to live. I want to thank You, Lord, that You have made me suitable for myself to know. I'm glad the remaking is not left to me, but that You are constantly at work in me, remolding me into the beautiful image You have planned for me.*

"Your hands made me and formed me.... You stoop down to make me great" (Psalm 119:73; 18:35). I am among those of whom it is written, "You are a chosen people, a royal priesthood, a holy nation, a people belonging to God" (1 Peter 2:9). Therefore I rejoice, knowing that You are in charge of my life, and my future holds only hope. "My heart is glad, and my glory rejoiceth; my flesh also shall rest in hope" (Psalm 16:9 KJV).

My Child, as you persistently draw upon spiritual resources, your life will continue to be one of joy and enthusiasm. Reflecting my glory, you are being transformed into my likeness with ever-increasing glory (2 Corinthians 3:18).

Letting go of your old negative thought patterns and accepting my truth about yourself has affected a transformation in you. Your affirmations in agreement with my Word sent new directions to your subconscious mind.

Thus you became like the hind whose front and back feet track together. Now that your subconscious is in agreement with your conscious mind, you are no longer a house divided against itself. You are becoming more and more a whole person, reflecting my glory.

᪥ ᪥ ᪥

Believe and Be

Lord, *I am constantly awed by the extremity of Your love. And the simplicity of Your grace amazes me. While I dash around looking for something to do for You, You say simply to believe and be.*

I see in Your Word that it has always been so. When the multitudes stormed You with such questions as, "What must we do to do the works God requires?" You surprised them by saying, "The work of God is this: to believe in the one he has sent" (John 6:28,29).

Then John wrote, "This is his command: to believe in the name of his son, Jesus Christ" (1 John 3:23). I was taught that Your commands consist of a long list of "shalts" and "shalt nots." But now I see that when we trust You and unreservedly live for You, rules and regulations take care of themselves. You dealt with everything on the cross. Now that I am in union with You, You live Your life through me. Thank You, Lord.

Yes, My Child, my invitation always has been and still is to enter my rest. I have already finished the work. My consuming desire is that my people would believe and become sharers of what I have accomplished. I want you to come to an "understanding and precise knowledge of every good thing that is [yours] in [your] identification with Christ Jesus—and unto His glory" (Philemon 1:6 AMP).

A Channel of Healing Love

Lord, what a privilege it was yesterday to be able to stand before that fellowship of ladies and proclaim Your healing love. Who would have dreamed that I who was hurting so badly a few years ago would now be speaking words of comfort to others?

With what validity the apostle Paul spoke when he said, "We have this treasure in jars of clay to show that this all-surpassing power is from God and not from us" (2 Corinthians 4:7)! I was a frail and broken clay pot. But You not only mended my brokenness but made me transparent enough to let Your light shine through. How exciting to know that the power which worked in me is now working through me to bring wholeness to the shattered.

You have permitted me to join the psalmist in declaring, "He heals the brokenhearted and binds up their wounds.... Great is our Lord and mighty in power; his understanding has no limit (Psalm 147:3,5).

My Child, now you have experienced the truth I spoke earlier: that nothing I do is wasted.

The psalmist did not pen empty words when he wrote, "The Lord is good to all; he has compassion on all he has made.... The Lord is faithful to all his promises and loving toward all he has made. The Lord upholds all those who fall and lifts up all who are bowed down" (Psalm 145:9,13,14).

A Garment of Praise

Lord, Your surprises never end. I find myself constantly being given opportunities to share the joy You have given me—that oil of joy that took the place of my heaviness. You indeed bestowed upon me a crown of beauty in place of ashes and a garment of praise in place of my rags of despair.

What a pleasure to be able to assure those who come to me that You who took my tattered clothes and replaced them with a robe of gladness will do the same for them. You do "not show favoritism" (Acts 10:34). Your blessings are for all. I'm glad I can tell everyone that You qualified them to share in the inheritance of the saints in the kingdom of light (Colossians 1:12), and that this inheritance begins here and now.

My Child, you have found out that my power and peace are available at all times and in all situations. You will continue to find it so. A large portion of that truth lies in the ability and willingness to praise me in all circumstances.

Just as the early Israelites could have reached their Promised Land much sooner if they had praised me instead of grumbling, so my children today more readily reach their land of promises when they praise me.

I supply the crowns of beauty and the garments of

praise. The responsibility of putting them on and wearing them rests with each individual. "Awake, awake, O Zion, clothe yourself with strength. Put on your garments of splendor" (Isaiah 52:1).

෴ ෴ ෴

Into His Light

Lord, You are so good to me! You have permitted me to have experiences revealing to me Your depth of love. You have given me revelations which have strengthened me immeasurably. I am most grateful for the inner experiences, the encounters deeper than the outward experiences I used to seek.

I thank You for teaching me how to be quiet in Your presence—how to achieve inner tranquility. That stillness accomplishes my receptivity to Your gifts of faith, hope, and love.

Your Word reminds me, "There is a time for everything" (Ecclesiastes 3:1). You have shown me that You not only fit everything into its proper schedule but that no activity or event is wasted. You use all things to bring glory to Your name and blessing to Your children.

How wonderful, Lord, that a person walking in Your Spirit "seldom reflects on the days of his life, because God keeps him occupied with gladness of heart" (Ecclesiastes 5:20). Your will is our joy. You said, "However many years a man may live, let him enjoy them all" (Ecclesiastes 11:8).

My Child, insights from my Word beyond intellectual understanding are my choice for all my children. And "to the man who pleases him, God gives wisdom, knowledge and happiness" (Ecclesiastes 2:26). Have you noticed that Solomon's theme in Ecclesiastes is that the only life with meaning is the life in which I am at center?

The outward manifestations of my presence are not to be despised, but the Christian who does not deprive himself of the deeper experiences and insights is the one growing in maturity. He has passed through a period of learning into a period of joyous progress.

You were "chosen, having been predestined according to the plan of him who works out everything in conformity with the purpose of his will" (Ephesians 1:11).

Now you have been brought out of darkness and into my kingdom of light. Continue therein and rejoice always.

⚜ ⚜ ⚜

Other Good
Harvest House Reading

THE QUIET HEART
by *June Masters Bacher*

This "quiet" daily devotional by June Masters Bacher, begins with a suggested Scripture reading, and through anecdotes, poetry, and prayer inspires each reader to see life with a fresh perspective. The *Quiet Hour*, a day-by-day "friend," encourages you to come to know God and learn how much richer knowing Him makes each day.

THE CONFIDENT WOMAN
by *Anabel Gillham*

Anabel Gillham was trying hard to be the total Christian woman—until she found out that's not what God wanted. Like Anabel, you may have tried hard to make your life work—and believed that if you tried hard enough to be the total Christian woman, God would honor your efforts. The liberating truth is that God does not want you to be a *total* Christian woman, but a *confident* Christian woman—one who is sure how much God loves and accepts her. Walk with Anabel as she shares how you can experience your *own* unshakable identity in Christ and find the strength to meet life's circumstances.

GOD CAN HEAL YOUR HEART
by *Marie Shropshire*

Marie Shropshire encourages people who are hurting with proof of the Lord's active interest in their lives and His power to heal. Each "letter from God" introduces an aspect of God's awesome nature.

THINGS HAPPEN WHEN WOMEN CARE
by *Emilie Barnes*

Things Happen When Women Care shows you how to carve out time for others by streamlining the details of daily living and home organization. This warm, insightful look at developing friendships and enlarging the boundaries of your personal ministry will give you the tools you need to start today on the great adventure of caring for others.

THE STAY-AT-HOME-MOM
by *Donna Otto*

Applauding the stay-at-home mom, author Donna Otto takes on the challenges and highlights the rewards of staying at home. With boundless enthusiasm for home and personal organization, Otto cheers on the stay-at-home mom and provides practical ideas to make the journey an adventure. This book will help you know whether being a stay-at-home mom is right for *you*.

GOD WHISPERS IN THE NIGHT
by *Marie Shropshire*

Depressed? Lonely? Concerned about the future? God has an answer. From the bestselling author of *In Touch with God* comes a sensitive, encouraging collection of heartfelt conversations between a hurting child and a caring heavenly Father. No matter what the challenge or the storm, Marie portrays with insightful accuracy the deepest feelings that penetrate our hearts and then helps us turn our focus back to God.

Dear Reader:

We would appreciate hearing from you regarding this Harvest House book. It will enable us to continue to give you the best in Christian publishing.

1. What most influenced you to purchase *In Touch with God*?
   ☐ Author ☐ Recommendations
   ☐ Subject matter ☐ Cover/Title
   ☐ Backcover copy ☐ _____

2. Where did you purchase this book?
   ☐ Christian bookstore ☐ Grocery store
   ☐ General bookstore ☐ Other
   ☐ Department store

3. Your overall rating of this book:
   ☐ Excellent ☐ Very good ☐ Good ☐ Fair ☐ Poor

4. How likely would you be to purchase other books by this author?
   ☐ Very likely ☐ Not very likely
   ☐ Somewhat likely ☐ Not at all

5. What types of books most interest you? (check all that apply)
   ☐ Women's books ☐ Fiction
   ☐ Marriage books ☐ Biographies
   ☐ Current issues ☐ Children's books
   ☐ Christian living ☐ Youth books
   ☐ Bible studies ☐ Other _____

6. Please check the box next to your age group.
   ☐ Under 18 ☐ 25–34 ☐ 45–54
   ☐ 18–24 ☐ 35–44 ☐ 55 and over

Mail to: Editorial Director
Harvest House Publishers
1075 Arrowsmith Rd.
Eugene, OR 97402-9197

Name _____

Address _____

City _____ State _____ Zip_____

Thank you for helping us to help you in future publications!